Teacher's Guide

Comprehension Plus

Dr. Diane Lapp
Dr. James Flood

Modern Curriculum Press

Program Reviewers

Carmen Arzt
Reading Recovery/Resource Teacher
LaPuente, California

Bonnie Nadick
Reading Specialist
Chicago, Illinois

Meg Ballantyne
Literacy (Reading) Specialist
Commerce City, Colorado

Sr. Mary Jean Raymond
Teacher/Educational Consultant
Cleveland, Ohio

Sharon Bonner
Literacy Resource Teacher
Glen Ridge, New Jersey

Bess Ann Sommers
Language Arts Consultant
Canton, Ohio

Alison Heath
Classroom Teacher
Houston, Texas

Fran Threewit
Reading Specialist
Kenwood, California

Carrie Jefferson
Teacher on Special Assignment
Antioch, California

Celebrity Authors

Cheryl Chapman, "Sam's Surprise," Lesson 9
J. Patrick Lewis, "Pete the Knight" and "Pete Meets the King," Lesson 20
Wendy Pfeffer, "What Makes Baby Teeth Fall Out?" and "Animal Teeth," Lesson 15
Robin Pulver, "Ups and Downs," Lesson 10
Susan L. Roth, "Who is Best?," Lesson 17
Anastasia Suen, "Space Race," Lesson 14

Program Development

Executive Editors: Leslie Feierstone-Barna, Magali Iglesias
Supervising Editor: Tisha Hamilton
Teacher's Guide Editor: David Stienecker
Design Development: MKR Design, New York, NY
Design: Karolyn Wehner
Illustrations: T14, T16, T18, T20, T22, T24, T26, T28, T30, T32: Jeff LeVan.
T15, T34: Elizabeth Allen. T71: P.T. Pie.

Copyright © 2002 by Pearson Education, Inc., publishing as Modern Curriculum Press, an imprint of Pearson Learning Group, 299 Jefferson Road, Parsippany, NJ 07054. All rights reserved. No part of this book may be reproduced or transmitted in any form or by any means, electronic, or mechanical, including photocopying, recording, or by any information storage and retrieval system, without permission in writing from the publisher. For information regarding permission(s), write to Rights and Permissions Department. This edition is published simultaneously in Canada by Pearson Education Canada.

ISBN: 0-7652-2186-1
Printed in the United States of America

15 16 17 18 19 V0YM 17 16 15 14 13

1-800-321-3106
www.pearsonlearning.com

Contents

Overview of Comprehension Plus T4
Using the Comprehension Plus Teacher's Guide T5
Using the Comprehension Plus Student Edition T6
Scope and Sequence of Skills T8
Skill Index Chart T9
Using the Comprehension Plus Tests T10
Tests Answer Key T11
Class Record-Keeping Chart T12
Progress Record Chart T13
Tests 1–6 . . . . .T14

Teacher's Guide Lessons

1	Following Directions	T38	13	Cause and Effect	T56
2	Using Details	T39	14	Real and Make-Believe	T57
3	Main Idea	T41	15	Using Context Clues	T59
4	Main Idea and Details	T42	16	Classifying	T60
5	Summarizing	T44	17	Comparing and Contrasting	T62
6	Drawing Conclusions	T45	18	Author's Purpose	T63
7	Drawing Conclusions	T47	19	Plot	T65
8	Sequence of Events	T48	20	Character	T66
9	Sequence of Events	T50	21	Setting	T68
10	Predicting Outcomes	T51	22	Alphabetizing	T69
11	Predicting Outcomes	T53	23	Picture Map	T71
12	Cause and Effect	T54	24	Picture and Bar Graphs	T72

Graphic Organizers Blackline Masters

Story Sequence Chart T74
Summarizing Chart T75
Prediction Chart T76
Main Ideas and Details Chart T77

Cause and Effect Chart T78
Venn Diagram T79
Sequence of Events .T80

Annotated Student Edition 81

Overview of COMPREHENSION PLUS

Comprehension Plus is a six-level comprehension program that provides explicit instruction and practice in major comprehension skills and strategies students need to derive meaning from written text. The Student's Editions and Teacher's Guides for grades 1–6 (Levels A–F) are designed to help students master the most frequently tested comprehension skills. *Comprehension Plus* provides another plus by giving students opportunities for application of comprehension skills in related study skill areas. For example, after students have developed skill in recognizing main idea and supporting details, they are given the opportunity to apply this skill to related study skills such as outlining, summarizing, paraphrasing, and using an encyclopedia.

Thorough Instruction

The basic lesson plan in *Comprehension Plus* provides another big plus. It is based on a simple, fundamental premise: Students can be taught the strategies that will help them comprehend written text. Recent studies have shown that in order to improve in a specific comprehension skill, students must be aware that the skill exists. They must also understand the dynamics involved in applying the skill in a meaningful context. Instruction directed to the students and accompanied by meaningful practice improves proficiency in comprehension.

The biggest plus in *Comprehension Plus* is that students are given much more than practice. They are given direct instruction in the strategy behind each comprehension skill as well as practice activities that allow them to apply the skill in a meaningful context.

Comprehensive Scope and Sequence

The focus skills that comprise the scope and sequence of *Comprehension Plus* are widely accepted as the most important comprehension skills students need to understand a variety of written texts. Students learn the skills that are tested on the following major standardized tests:

- Stanford Achievement Test (SAT-9)
- California Achievement Test (CAT-5)
- TerraNova
- California Test of Basic Skills (CTBS-5)
- Iowa Test of Basic Skills (ITBS-M)
- Metropolitan Achievement Test (MAT-7)
- National Assessment of Educational Progress

The Skills Index on page T9 of every Teacher's Guide provides a complete listing of every focus skill and maintenance skill and lists the lesson in which the skill can be found.

Range of Text Difficulty

All reading passages included in *Comprehension Plus* have been evaluated using either the Spache or Dale-Chall formula for determining text difficulty. The following chart provides the range for each level of the program.

Comprehension Plus Level	Grade Level	Range of Text Difficulty Formula	Range of Scores
A	1	Spache	1.0 – 1.6
B	2	Spache	1.8 – 2.6
C	3	Spache	2.8 – 3.6
D	4	Spache	3.8 – 4.6
E	5	Dale-Chall	4.8 – 5.6
F	6	Dale-Chall	5.8 – 6.6

Comprehension Plus • Level A

Using the COMPREHENSION PLUS Teacher's Guide

The Teacher's Guide has everything you need to help students learn and practice the comprehension strategies, study skills, and word study skills they need to succeed. Carefully sequenced instruction, application of focus skills, maintenance skills, and assessment tests help students master the key comprehension skills and strategies necessary for them to understand written text.

Focus Skill
- The focus skill and instructional objective are clearly presented at the beginning of each lesson.

Teaching Tips
- Provide valuable information about the purpose for teaching each skill.
- Help you pinpoint students' understanding of each focus skill.

Reviewed and Maintained Skills
- Two or three comprehension skills, one phonics skill, and one writing skill are maintained within each lesson.

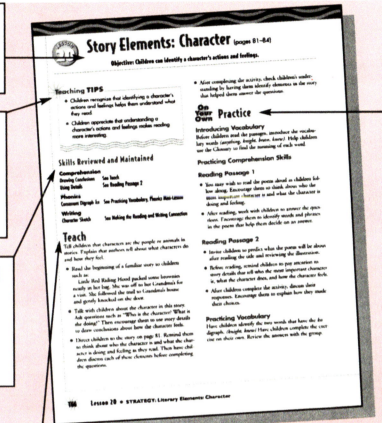

On Your Own Practice
Easy-to-use teaching tips help you assign and assess practice opportunities:
- **Introducing Vocabulary**
Aids students' understanding of the passages by preteaching the key words.
- **Practicing Comprehension Skills**
Reading the Passages
Provides tips and activities for guiding students through the reading passages and learning the focus skill.
- **Practicing Vocabulary**
Reviews key words in each passage and identifies the words that focus on the featured word study or phonics skill.

Teach
A quick, step-by-step mini-lesson for teaching the focus skill through interactive activities.
- The skill is presented or modeled for the student through a familiar, real-life example.
- Students get a first-hand opportunity to interact with the focus skill while completing the activity with the teacher.

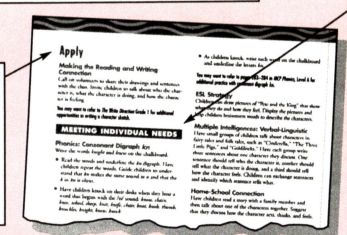

On Your Own Apply
Helpful suggestions for reviewing and evaluating students' writing, as well as cross-references to related lessons in **Modern Curriculum Press's The Write Direction,** reinforce the reading-writing connection.

Meeting Individual Needs
Support your students' diverse needs with meaningful activities that interest all students. Each lesson includes
- an activity that reviews the phonics maintenance skill.
- an activity that makes the lesson more accessible to students acquiring English.
- an activity that addresses one or more of the Multiple Intelligences.
- a simple activity related to the focus skill for students to take home and share with family members.

Comprehension Plus • Level A

Using the COMPREHENSION PLUS Student Edition

Student-friendly and designed to create meaningful reading experiences, each lesson in the Student Editions is designed to help students master a skill in context.

Easy as 1-2-3. Teach. Check for Understanding. Practice.

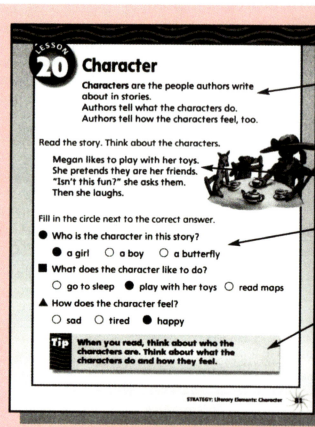

Direct Instruction
Clear, student-friendly instruction introduces students to the focus skill.

Guided Practice
- Students are guided through a brief passage that clearly illustrates the skill.
- Students then have an opportunity to apply the learning through a short practice activity.

Tip
A helpful tip reinforces instruction and helps students remember how to recognize and use the skill.

On Your Own Reading Passages 1 and 2
- High-interest reading passages engage readers immediately.
- These are stories and articles your students will want to read, covering a wide variety of fictional and nonfictional genres.

Celebrity Authors
Several selections in each level have been written by well-known trade book authors, such as J. Patrick Lewis, Trinka Hakes Noble, Anne Hodgman, Norma Johnston, Reeve Lindbergh, and more.

Comprehension Plus • Level A

Practicing Comprehension Skills

- Students practice and solidify their understanding of the focus skill through a variety of activities, including multiple choice, question and answer, written response, and graphic organizers.
- The variety of practice formats motivates students to master the skills.

Read the poem. Think about who the main character is.

Pete Meets the King
by J. Patrick Lewis

The King was brave. The King was kind.
He walked along the street.
"Good day. How do you do?"
he'd say to people he would meet.
He knew today he'd meet a knight.
The knight he met was Pete!

Draw a line under the correct answer.

4. Who is the most important character?
   Pete   a horse   the King

5. What does the King do that shows he likes people?
   The King asks people to visit his castle.
   The King shows people his horse.
   The King says, "Good day" to people.

6. How do you think the King feels as he walks down the street?
   sleepy   silly   happy

STRATEGY: Literary Elements: Character

---

7. Which words tell about the King? Write the words on the line.
   tired and hungry   brave and kind   loud and wild

   The king is _____brave and kind_____ .

Practicing Vocabulary

Draw a line from the sentence to the word.

8. The ____ rode on his horse. — anything
9. He would do ____ the king asked. — knight
10. He was very ____. — brave
11. He ____ the king was his friend. — knew

 On another sheet of paper, draw a picture of a story character you like. Then write two or three sentences about the character.

Lesson 20

Practicing Vocabulary

- Students practice key words from the passage through a variety of exercise formats.
- A Glossary, containing these words and their definitions, is included at the end of the Student Edition.

Making the Reading and Writing Connection

- Connecting to the lesson topic and the focus skill, writing activities motivate students to apply their knowledge as they use a variety of writing forms.

Comprehension Plus • Level A

Scope and Sequence

The following chart shows the Focus Skills with a ☆ symbol and the Maintenance Skills with a ★ symbol. A more detailed Skills Index is provided in the Teacher's Guide for each level.

LEVEL	A	B	C	D	E	F
COMPREHENSION						
Strategies and Skills						
Activating prior knowledge			★			
Analyzing		★	★			
Author's purpose	☆	☆	☆★	☆★	☆★	☆★
Author's viewpoint			☆	☆	☆	☆
Cause and effect	☆★	☆★	☆★	☆★	☆★	☆★
Classifying	☆★	☆★	★			
Comparing and contrasting	☆★	☆★	☆★	☆★	☆★	☆★
Context clues to determine meaning	☆	☆	☆★	☆	☆	☆
Details	☆★		★			
Drawing conclusions	☆★	☆★	☆★	☆★	☆★	☆★
Expressing opinions		★	★			
Fact and opinion		☆	☆★	☆	☆	☆
Fantasy and realism	☆	☆	☆			
Hypothesizing		★	★			
Main idea	☆★	☆★	☆★	☆★	☆★	☆★
Making generalizations		★	☆	☆★	☆	☆★
Making inferences			★			★
Making judgments about ideas and text			☆★	☆★	☆★	☆★
Outlining and Notetaking					☆	☆★
Paraphrasing		☆	☆	☆	☆	☆
Personal opinions			★			
Persuasive devices and propaganda					☆	☆
Point of view		☆	☆	☆	☆	☆
Predicting outcomes	☆★	☆★	☆★	☆★	☆★	☆
Problem and solution			★			
Sequence: order of events	☆★	☆	☆★	☆★	☆	☆
Sequence: steps in a process	★	☆	☆	☆	☆	☆
Summarizing	☆	☆★	☆★	☆★	☆★	☆★
Supporting details		☆★	☆	☆★	☆★	☆★
Synthesizing information			★			
Text structure: method			☆	☆	☆	☆
Visualizing	★	★	★			★
Story Structure						
Character	☆	☆★	☆★	☆★	☆★	☆
Plot	☆★	☆	☆★	☆	☆★	☆★
Setting	☆	☆	☆	☆	☆★	☆★
Theme		☆	☆	☆	☆★	☆
Word Study						
Alphabetizing	☆	☆				
Analogies						☆★
Antonyms		☆	☆	☆	☆	☆
Compound words		☆	★			
Connotation and denotation				☆	☆	☆
Figurative language: simile and metaphor			☆	☆		
Homonyms		☆			☆	
Synonyms		☆	☆	☆	☆	☆
Suffixes			★			

LEVEL	A	B	C	D	E	F
Using figurative language					☆	☆
RESEARCH AND STUDY SKILLS						
Charts and tables		☆	☆	☆	☆	☆
Dictionary		☆	☆★	☆	☆	☆
Encyclopedia			☆	☆	☆	☆
Following directions	☆★					
Graphs	☆	☆	☆	☆	☆	☆
Library card catalog/the Internet					☆	☆
Maps		☆	☆	☆	☆	☆
Picture maps and clues	☆★					
WRITING						
Article			★			★
Bar graph	★					
Book report		★	★			
Campaign speech						★
Cause and effect sentences	★					
Character sketch	★	★	★			★
Compare and contrast paragraph			★	★		
Description			★	★		★
Description of a setting			★	★		
Descriptive paragraph			★		★	★
Dictionary page					★	
Directions			★		★	★
Eyewitness account						★
Fantasy			★	★	★	★
Graph			★			
How-to paragraph			★	★		
Informative paragraph		★	★	★		
Journal entry		★	★	★		★
Label Book	★					
Letter		★	★		★	★
Log entry			★			
Myth					★	★
Movie review						★
Narrative paragraph			★	★	★	★
News report			★		★	
Note		★	★			
Paragraph			★	★		★
Persuasive paragraph				★		★
Picture map	★					
Poem		★	★		★	
Poster			★			
Realistic story						★
Riddles	★		★			
Sentences	★	★				
Sentences that compare	★					
Story		★	★			★
Summary			★	★		★
Tongue twister		★				

T8   **Comprehension Plus • Level A**

Skills Index

The following chart shows the lessons where the Focus Skills and the Maintenance Skills are presented in the Student's Edition and Teacher's Guide of Level A.

The first column lists the skills. The second column lists in boldface type the lesson numbers where the Focus Skills are presented. The third column lists the lesson numbers where the Maintenance Skills are presented.

Each Focus Skill is presented in the Strategy section of the lesson in the Student's Edition. The "On Your Own" section, which begins with a reading selection, provides further opportunities to apply the Focus Skill to a new context. The Maintenance Skills included in each lesson are those skills that were presented as Focus Skills in other lessons in Level A.

Strategies and Skills	Focus Skills	Maintenance Skills
Comprehension		
Author's purpose	**18**	
Cause and effect	**12, 13**	7, 21
Classifying	**16**	22
Comparing and contrasting	**17**	21
Drawing conclusions	**6, 7**	4, 9, 14, 15, 16, 17, 20, 22
Main idea	**3**	
Main idea and details	**4**	5, 6, 7, 8, 10, 12, 13, 14, 24
Making predictions		2, 5, 9, 12, 17, 18
Predicting		3
Predicting outcomes	**10, 11**	
Real and make-believe	**14**	
Realism and fantasy		4, 19
Sequence		19
Sequence of events	**8, 9**	10, 13, 18
Sequence: Steps in a process		1
Summarizing	**5**	
Using context clues	**15**	
Using details	**2**	3, 11, 15, 16, 20, 23, 24
Visualizing		11
Story Structure		
Plot	**19**	23
Character	**20**	
Setting	**21**	
Word Study		
Alphabetizing	**22**	
Research and Study Skills		
Following directions	**1**	3, 8
Picture clues		2, 6
Picture map	**23**	
Picture and bar graphs	**24**	
Using picture clues		1

Comprehension Plus • Level A   T9

Using the Comprehension Plus Tests

Assessment Tests are provided in the Teacher's Guide for each level of the program. There are six tests in Level A, five tests in Levels B–D, and six tests in Levels E and F. Each test is designed to measure students' proficiency on four to six skills taught at each level. The tests may be used as pretests or posttests depending on the students' needs and the teacher's instructional style. If students answer two out of the three tested items correctly, they are considered to have mastered that skill.

In addition to the tests, *Comprehension Plus* provides the following management tools:
- Class Record-Keeping Chart (page T12)
- Progress Record Chart (page T13)

There are a total of six tests offered for this level of *Comprehension Plus*. You may want to use them to evaluate how well students have mastered the 24 focus skills taught in the lessons. As the following chart summarizes, each test includes two passages. Students will answer six comprehension questions for each passage. Each set of six questions will test students' understanding of two focus skills.

To administer the test:

- Make as many copies of a test as you need.

- Have students write their names on each page.

- Explain that students will read two test passages and answer six questions for each passage.

- After students read the first passage, you may want to review their answers to the first test item to make certain they understand what is expected of them.

- Use the Answer Key on page T11 to score each test.

- You may want to record the test results on the Class Record-Keeping Chart on page T12.

Test	Passage Number	Lessons	Skills
1	1	1 & 2	• Following Directions • Using Details
	2	3 & 5	• Main Idea • Summarizing
2	1	4 & 6	• Main Idea and Details • Drawing Conclusions
	2	7 & 8	• Drawing Conclusions • Sequence of Events
3	1	9 & 10	• Sequence of Events • Predicting Outcomes
	2	11 & 12	• Predicting Outcomes • Cause and Effect
4	1	13 & 14	• Cause and Effect • Real and Make-Believe
	2	15 & 16	• Using Context Clues • Classifying
5	1	17 & 18	• Comparing and Contrasting • Author's Purpose
	2	19 & 22	• Plot • Alphabetizing
6	1	21 & 23	• Setting • Picture Map
	2	20 & 24	• Character • Picture and Bar Graphs

T10   Comprehension Plus • Level A

Answer Key

Test 1 (Passages 1 and 2 numbered sequentially)
1. **picnic** Using details
2. **basket** Using details
3. **run and play** Using details
4. **Circle bread and honey.** Following directions
5. **Draw a line under blanket.** Following directions
6. **Draw an X on the ball.** Following directions
7. **fur** Main idea
8. **lumps and bumps** Main idea
9. **hard** Main idea
10. **all animals** Summarizing
11. **Animals wear different kinds of coats.** Summarizing
12. **Animal Coats** Main idea

Test 2 (Passages 1 and 2 numbered sequentially)
1. **balloon** Main idea and details
2. **people** Drawing conclusions
3. **hot air** Main idea and details
4. **in the evening** Drawing conclusions
5. **a pool** Drawing conclusions
6. **People take rides in hot air balloons.** Main idea and details
7. **lake** Drawing conclusions
8. **fish** Drawing conclusions
9. **puts a worm on it** Sequence of events
10. **throws his line in the water** Sequence of events
11. **waits for fish** Sequence of events
12. **bored** Drawing conclusions

Test 3 (Passages 1 and 2 numbered sequentially)
1. **first** Sequence of events
2. **Simon Says** Sequence of events
3. **The ants hear "R-r-roar!"** Sequence of events
4. **play a game in the tree** Predicting outcomes
5. **run back to the grass** Predicting outcomes
6. **run up the tree** Predicting outcomes
7. **they won't look the same** Cause and effect
8. **she bit into an apple** Cause and effect
9. **Pam's tooth came out** Cause and effect
10. **look at Pam's tooth** Predicting outcomes

Test 4 (Passages 1 and 2 numbered sequentially)
1. **it feels good** Cause and effect
2. **goes up high** Cause and effect
3. **they like the show** Cause and effect
4. **a trunk** Real and make-believe
5. **talk** Real and make-believe
6. **make-believe story** Real and make-believe
7. **many people** Classifying
8. **animals** Classifying
9. **buildings** Classifying
10. **still** Context clues
11. **loud** Context clues
12. **active** Context clues

Test 5 (Passages 1 and 2 numbered sequentially)
1. **Sandy Snowball** Author's purpose
2. **snow and sand** Author's purpose
3. **to tell you about snow and sand** Author's purpose
4. **You can run in both.** Comparing and contrasting
5. **Only sand is dry.** Comparing and contrasting
6. **only snow** Comparing and contrasting
7. **at the end of the story** Plot
8. **The children find things to play.** Plot
9. **at the beginning of the story** Plot
10. **box** Alphabetizing
11. **pot** Alphabetizing
12. **box, can, pot** Alphabetizing

Test 6 (Passages 1 and 2 numbered sequentially)
1. **farm** Setting
2. **day** Setting
3. **summer** Setting
4. **at the house** Picture map
5. **the cow** Picture map
6. **by the tree** Picture map
7. **Toad** Character
8. **sad** Character
9. **a make-believe animal** Character
10. **4** Picture and bar graphs
11. **2** Picture and bar graphs
12. **mouse** Picture and bar graphs

Comprehension Plus • Level A 111

Class Record-Keeping Chart

The following chart can be used to record the number of items each student has answered correctly for each skill tested. Students need to answer correctly two out of the three tested items per skill to be considered to have mastered that skill. Write in each cell the number of items answered correctly by the student. Add the total of correct answers in the bottom cells.

Name

Test	Items	Strategies and Skills									
1	1–3	Using details									
	4–6	Following directions									
	7–9, 12	Main idea									
	10–11	Summarizing									
2	1, 3, 6	Main idea and details									
	2, 4–5	Drawing conclusions									
	7–8, 12	Drawing conclusions									
	9–11	Sequence of events									
3	1–3	Sequence of events									
	4–6	Predicting outcomes									
	7–9	Cause and effect									
	10	Predicting outcomes									
4	1–3	Cause and effect									
	4–6	Real and make-believe									
	7–9	Classifying									
	10–12	Using context clues									
5	1–3	Author's purpose									
	4–6	Comparing and contrasting									
	7–9	Plot									
	10–12	Alphabetizing									
6	1–3	Setting									
	4–6	Picture map									
	7–9	Character									
	10–12	Picture and bar graphs									
		Total Correct									

T12   Comprehension Plus • Level A

Progress Record Chart

Name_____

The following chart can be used to record students' progress upon completion of the Comprehension/Study Skills, the Vocabulary Skill, and the Writing Skill activities for each lesson. The symbol ✔, +, or – can be used or any numerical system devised by the teacher to indicate students' work as satisfactory (✔), very good (+), or needs improvement (–). Page references for each Strategy and Skill are provided for convenient reference.

Lesson	Focus Skill	Comprehension Study Skills		Vocabulary Skills		Writing Skills	
		PAGE	✔, +, –	PAGE	✔, +, –	PAGE	✔, +, –
1	Following directions	5–7		8		8	
2	Using details	9–11		12		12	
3	Main idea	13–15		16		16	
4	Main idea and details	17–19		20		20	
5	Summarizing	21–23		24		24	
6	Drawing conclusions	25–27		28		28	
7	Drawing conclusions	29–31		32		32	
8	Sequence of events	33–35		36		36	
9	Sequence of events	37–39		40		40	
10	Predicting outcomes	41–43		44		44	
11	Predicting outcomes	45–47		48		48	
12	Cause and effect	49–51		52		52	
13	Cause and effect	53–55		56		56	
14	Real and make-believe	57–59		60		60	
15	Using context clues	61–63		64		64	
16	Classifying	65–67		68		68	
17	Comparing and contrasting	69–71		72		72	
18	Author's purpose	73–75		76		76	
19	Plot	77–79		80		80	
20	Character	81–83		84		84	
21	Setting	85–87		88		88	
22	Alphabetizing	89–91		92		92	
23	Picture map	93–95		96		96	
24	Picture and bar graphs	97–99		100		100	

Comprehension Plus • Level A

Name _____ TEST 1

Read the story below. Then answer the questions on the next page.

Bear Family Fun

"Let's get ready for a picnic," said Mother Bear.
Father Bear can get a big basket.
Sister Bear can put bread and honey in the basket.
Brother Bear can find a blanket.
Baby Bear can bring his ball.
After the picnic, we can run and play.

Comprehension Plus • Level A

Name _____ TEST 1, continued

Fill in the circle next to the word or words that complete each sentence.

1. This story tells about bears getting ready for a _____.
   ○ birthday   ○ picnic   ○ trip

2. Father Bear can get a big _____.
   ○ basket   ○ car   ○ box

3. After the picnic, the bears will _____.
   ○ sing and dance   ○ sit and sleep   ○ run and play

4. What food can Sister Bear bring? Draw a circle around the picture.

5. What can Brother Bear find? Draw a line under the picture.

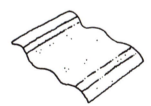  

6. What will Baby Bear bring? Draw an X on the picture.

Comprehension Plus • Level A

Name _____ TEST 1, continued

Read the story below. Then answer the questions below and on the next page.

Animals wear different kinds of coats.
Dogs and cats wear fur coats.
A toad's coat has lumps and bumps.
A turtle wears a hard coat.
All animals wear coats.
They just can't hang them up!

Fill in the circle next to the word or words that complete each sentence.

7. Dogs and cats wear _____ coats.
   ○ fur   ○ feather   ○ grass

Comprehension Plus • Level A

Name _____ **TEST 1,** *continued*

8. A toad's coat has _____.

    ○ dots and spots

    ○ lumps and bumps

    ○ pretty colors

9. A turtle's coat is _____.

    ○ red   ○ soft   ○ hard

Fill in the circle next to the words that answer each question.

10. Which animals wear coats?

    ○ all animals

    ○ some animals

    ○ one animal

11. What important thing do the sentences tell?

    ○ Animals wear different kinds of coats.

    ○ People can hang up their coats.

    ○ Some animals wear fur coats.

12. What is the best name for the story?

    ○ Buying a Coat

    ○ All Kinds of Animals

    ○ Animal Coats

Comprehension Plus • Level A

Name _____ TEST 2

Read the story below. Then answer the questions on the next page.

Balloon Ride

The sun is going down.
A big balloon takes us up!
This balloon does not pop.
It is filled with hot air.
We are standing in a basket.
When we look up, we see our balloon.
When we look down, we see people.
The people are playing in the water.
We wave to the people, and they
wave back.

T18 Comprehension Plus • Level A

Name _____ **TEST 2,** *continued*

Fill in the circle next to the word or words that complete each sentence.

1. This story tells about riding in a ____.
   ○ car   ○ balloon   ○ train

2. The basket holds _____.
   ○ people   ○ balloons   ○ food

3. The balloon is filled with _____.
   ○ hot air   ○ water   ○ popcorn

Fill in the circle next to the words that answer each question.

4. When do the people go for a ride?
   ○ in the morning

   ○ in the afternoon

   ○ in the evening

5. What is the balloon flying over?
   ○ a school   ○ a pool   ○ a building

6. Which sentence tells what the story is about?
   ○ People are playing in the water.

   ○ People take rides in hot air balloons.

   ○ Some balloons do not pop.

Comprehension Plus • **Level A**   T19

Name _____ **TEST 2,** *continued*

Read the story below. Then answer the questions on the next page.

Some Catch!

"Maybe we will catch something here," Grandpa said to Luke.
"I will help you get your pole ready."
"First put a worm on your line."
"Next throw the line into the water."
"Then I wait!" said Luke.
Two hours later Luke was still waiting.
"Have you caught anything yet?" asked Grandpa.
"All I'm going to catch is a cold!" said Luke.

Name _____ **TEST 2,** *continued*

Fill in the circle next to the word or words that complete each sentence.

7. Luke and Grandpa are at a _____.
   - ○ store
   - ○ lake
   - ○ garden

8. Luke and Grandpa want to catch a ____.
   - ○ ball
   - ○ butterfly
   - ○ fish

Fill in the circle next to the words that answer each question.

9. What does Luke do first to his line?
   - ○ throws it in the water
   - ○ puts it in the car
   - ○ puts a worm on it

10. What does Luke do next?
    - ○ throws his line in the water
    - ○ waits for fish
    - ○ tells a joke

11. What does Luke do after he throws his line in the water?
    - ○ gets a worm
    - ○ talks to Grandpa
    - ○ waits for fish

12. How does Luke feel at the end of the story?
    - ○ excited
    - ○ afraid
    - ○ bored

Comprehension Plus ● Level A

Name _____ TEST 3

Read the story below. Then answer the questions on the next page.

Ants Play "Simon Says"

Some ants like to play games. First, they find a spot in the grass. Then, one ant shouts, "Simon says, walk." All the ants walk. The ant says, "Jump." None of the ants jump. Next, the ants hear "R-r-roar!" Dad is going to cut the grass. The ant says, **"Run!"** All the ants run up a tree!

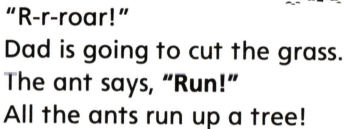

Comprehension Plus • Level A

Name _____ **TEST 3,** *continued*

Fill in the circle next to the word or words that complete each sentence.

1. The ants find a spot in the grass _____.

○ first   ○ next   ○ last

2. Then the ants play _____.

○ hide-and-seek   ○ ball games   ○ Simon Says

Fill in the circle next to the words that answer each question.

3. The ants are playing a game. What happens next?

○ The ants cut the grass.

○ The ants jump.   ○ The ants hear "R-r-roar!"

4. The ants are safe in the tree. What do you think they will do?

○ play a game in the tree

○ run down the tree   ○ play in the grass

5. After Dad leaves, what do you think the ants will do?

○ climb higher in the tree

○ look for other ants   ○ run back to the grass

6. What do you think the ants will do if they hear "R-r-roar" again?

○ run up the tree

○ play Simon Says   ○ say "R-r-roar"

Comprehension Plus ● Level A   **23**

Name _____ **TEST 3,** continued

Read the story below. Then answer the questions on the next page.

Our Two Front Teeth

Penny and Pam are twins.
They look the same.
Their front baby teeth are ready to fall out.
"I'm going to pull my tooth," said Penny.
"No!" said Pam.
"Then you won't look like me."
"I'll wait," said Penny.
Then Pam bit into an apple.
"My tooth came out!" yelled Pam.
Now the twins look different.

Comprehension Plus • Level A

Name _____ **TEST 3,** *continued*

Fill in the circle next to the word or words that complete each sentence.

7. Pam does not want Penny to pull her tooth because _____.

   ○ they won't look the same

   ○ they want to eat lunch

   ○ they both have baby teeth

8. Pam's tooth came out because _____.

   ○ she pulled it out

   ○ she had a twin sister

   ○ she bit into an apple

9. The twins look different now because _____.

   ○ Pam likes apples

   ○ Pam's tooth came out

   ○ Pam has baby teeth

10. What do you think Penny will do next?

    ○ eat lunch

    ○ look at Pam's tooth

    ○ walk away

Comprehension Plus ● **Level A**   125

Name _____ TEST 4

Read the story below. Then answer the questions on the next page.

Dancing Elephants

Kara and Sara Elephant love to dance!
"I love to turn around because it feels good!" said Kara.
"I love to leap so I go high into the air," said Sara.
At the dance show Kara turned fast. She could not stop.
Sara leaped high. She stopped Kara with her trunk.
The people clapped for Kara and Sara.

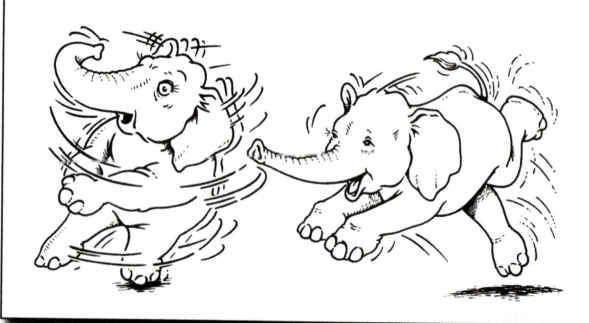

Comprehension Plus • Level A

Name _____ **TEST 4,** *continued*

Fill in the circle next to the word or words that complete each sentence.

1. Kara likes to turn around because _____.
   ○ she goes up   ○ she never falls   ○ it feels good

2. When Sara leaps she _____.
   ○ goes up high   ○ claps her hands   ○ turns around

3. The people clap because _____.
   ○ they like to dance
   ○ they don't like Sara
   ○ they like the show

4. A real elephant has _____
   ○ a trunk   ○ a dress   ○ dancing shoes

5. Real elephants can not _____.
   ○ move   ○ turn   ○ talk

6. This is a _____.
   ○ real story
   ○ make-believe story
   ○ sad story

Comprehension Plus ● **Level A**

Name _____ TEST 4, continued

Read the story below. Then answer the questions on the next page.

City or Country

People live in the city and the country.
The city is a noisy place. You hear car horns honking.
There are many busy people all around you.
You see tall buildings and big buses.
The country is a quiet and calm place.
There are not many people.
You see fields, animals, and only a few buildings.
Where would you like to live?

Comprehension Plus • Level A

Name _____ **TEST 4,** *continued*

Fill in the circle next to the word or words that complete each sentence.

7. The city has ____.

○ many fields

○ many animals

○ many people

8. The country has ____.

○ big buses   ○ animals   ○ tall buildings

9. The city has more ____.

○ buildings   ○ animals   ○ fields

Fill in the circle next to the word that means the same as the underlined word.

10. The country is a quiet and <u>calm</u> place.

○ still   ○ friendly   ○ exciting

11. The city is a <u>noisy</u> place. You hear car horns honking.

○ loud   ○ quiet   ○ pretty

12. There are many <u>busy</u> people are all around you.

○ friendly   ○ active   ○ happy

Comprehension Plus • Level A

Name _____ **TEST 5**

Read the poem below. Then answer the questions on the next page.

Snow and Sand
by Sandy Snowball

Snow and sand are places to play.
So where will you have fun today?
Snow is wet, and sand is dry.
Only snow falls from the sky.
Make a castle in snow or sand.
Taste fresh snow, but never sand.
On the ground, in sand and snow.
You can run—Get ready, set, go!

130 Comprehension Plus • Level A

Name _____ **TEST 5,** *continued*

Fill in the circle next to the words that answer each question.

1. Who wrote this poem?

   ○ Snow White   ○ U. R. Funny   ○ Sandy Snowball

2. What is the poem about?

   ○ making castles

   ○ snow and sand   ○ places to play

3. Why do you think the author wrote "Snow and Sand"?

   ○ to tell you how to make a sand castle

   ○ to tell you what to taste

   ○ to tell you about snow and sand

4. How are snow and sand alike?

   ○ You can get wet in both.

   ○ You can run in both.   ○ You can taste both.

5. How are snow and sand different?

   ○ Only sand is on the ground.

   ○ Only snow is on the ground.

   ○ Only sand is dry.

6. What does this sentence tell about? "It falls from the sky."

   ○ only sand   ○ only snow   ○ both snow and sand

Comprehension Plus ● **Level A**   **31**

Name _____ TEST 5, continued

Read the story below. Then answer the questions on the next page.

Play in the ABC Parade

The children on ABC Street wanted to have a parade.

"Let's look for things to play," said Ben.

Tom finds a paper box.

Sal uses an empty can.

Carrie gets a pot.

"We can line up in ABC order," said Ben. "We will make ABC music on ABC Street!"

Comprehension Plus • Level A

Name _____ **TEST 5,** *continued*

Fill in the circle next to the words that answer each question.

7. When do the children line up in ABC order?
- ○ at the beginning of the story
- ○ in the middle of the story
- ○ at the end of the story

8. What happens in the middle of the story?
- ○ The children make music.
- ○ The children find things to play.
- ○ The children sing and dance.

9. When do the children decide to have a parade?
- ○ at the beginning of the story
- ○ in the middle of the story
- ○ at the end of the story

10. Which word comes first in ABC order?
- ○ can
- ○ box
- ○ pot

11. Which word comes last in ABC order?
- ○ pot
- ○ box
- ○ can

12. Which group of words is in ABC order?
- ○ box, can, pot
- ○ can, box, pot
- ○ pot, box, can

Comprehension Plus • Level A 133

Name _____ **TEST 6**

Read the story below. Then answer the questions on the next page.

Hunt for the Hive

Bobby Bee was lost. He could not find his hive.

"Have you seen my hive?" Bobby asked the dog.

The dog told Bobby to ask the cow.

The cow told Bobby to ask the horse.

"Have you seen my hive?" Bobby asked the horse.

"Yes. Listen for a bird. You will find your hive," said the horse.

Comprehension Plus • Level A

Name _____ **TEST 6,** continued

Fill in the circle next to the word or words that complete each sentence.

1. This story happens on a _____.
   ○ mountain   ○ farm   ○ beach

2. Bobby is looking for his hive during the ____.
   ○ night   ○ storm   ○ day

3. This story happens in the _____.
   ○ summer   ○ winter   ○ fall

Look at the picture map. Fill in the circle next to the words that answer each question.

4. Where does Bobby talk to the dog?
   ○ at the house
   ○ at the tree
   ○ in the field

5. What animal is in the barn?
   ○ the horse   ○ the cow   ○ the dog

6. Where will Bobby find his hive?
   ○ in the house
   ○ in the barn
   ○ by the tree

Comprehension Plus ● Level A   135

Name _____ TEST 6, continued

Read the story below. Then answer the questions on the next page.

Pond Friends

Toad was crying. He had no friends.
"I will look for a new home and new friends," he said.
Toad came to a beautiful pond.
He counted many fish, ducks, and even a mouse.
They showed Toad a nice grassy spot.
Toad smiled as his pond friends helped him move.

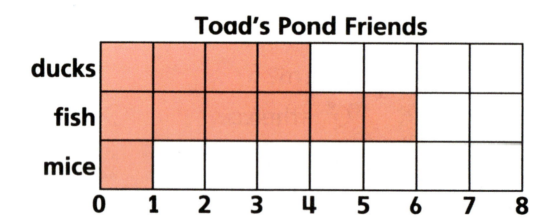

Name _____ **TEST 6,** *continued*

Fill in the circle next to the words that answer each question.

7. Who is the main character in this story?

   ○ a girl　　　○ Toad　　　○ the pond

8. How does Toad feel at the beginning of the story?

   ○ happy　　　○ tired　　　○ sad

9. How would you describe Toad?

   ○ a make-believe animal

   ○ a real animal

   ○ someone's pet

Look at the bar graph. Fill in the circle next to the number that answers each question.

10. How many ducks are at the pond?

    ○ 7　　　　　　○ 1　　　　　　○ 4

11. How many more fish are there than ducks?

    ○ 3　　　　　　○ 1　　　　　　○ 2

Fill in the circle next to the word that finishes this sentence.

12. Toad sees only one _____

    ○ mouse　　　○ duck　　　○ fish

Comprehension Plus ● Level A

Lesson 1: Following Directions (pages 5–8)

Objective: Children can follow oral and written directions.

Teaching TIPS

- Children become better independent readers by learning how to follow directions.
- Children take notice of specific school- and book-related direction words.

Skills Reviewed and Maintained

Comprehension
Sequence: Steps in a Process — See Reading Passage 1
Using Picture Clues — See Reading Passage 2

Phonics
Short *a* — See Practicing Vocabulary, Phonics Mini-Lesson

Writing
Sentences — See Making the Reading and Writing Connection

Teach

Trace around your hand on the chalkboard. Write the words *hand* and *nose* under the picture and read these words aloud.

- Ask a volunteer to draw a circle around the word that goes with the picture.
- Tell children that you just gave them a direction to follow. Then give other directions for the hand picture: Draw a ring on the little finger. Draw a circle around the thumb. Trace your hand next to my hand. Draw fingernails on the hand.
- Point out to children that they read directions every day at home and at school. Have children brainstorm directions they hear, for example: Please get out your pencil. Walk, don't run, in the hall. Brush your teeth. Put on your pajamas.
- Next, have children look at the pictures on page 5. Ask them to read the directions that the dad is giving his son.
- Read the directions aloud for each exercise at the bottom of the page. Be sure children understand and are following the directions.
- Read aloud the direction words in the tip. Check for understanding by having children demonstrate each direction as you say it.

On Your Own Practice

Introducing Vocabulary

Before children read the sentences, introduce the vocabulary words *(sand, catch, water, worm)* and discuss their meanings. Introduce the Glossary to children and help them use the Glossary to find the definitions of the words.

Practicing Comprehension Skills

Reading Passage 1

- Have children read "Fun in the Sand." Provide children an opportunity to practice sequencing events by asking them to identify what they would do first, next, and last.
- Tell children to read the directions carefully before they answer each question. As you review the answers, have children explain what the directions asked them to do for each exercise.

Reading Passage 2

- Ask children to use the clues provided in the picture to describe what is happening on page 7. Then have them read the title. Have children predict what the sentences in "Let's Go Fishing" will be about.
- After reading the story, have children identify direction words in the exercises.
- Direct children to complete the exercises. Discuss the answers together.

Practicing Vocabulary

Have children identify the vocabulary words that have the short *a* sound. *(sand, catch)* Then direct children to complete the vocabulary exercise independently. Review the answers with the class.

Lesson 1 • STRATEGY: Following Directions

Apply

Making the Reading and Writing Connection

Ask volunteers to show their beach picture and read their sentence. Then ask each child to follow a direction using his or her picture, such as "Point to the sun." or "Count the fish in the water."

You may want to refer to *The Write Direction* Grade 1 for additional opportunities in writing sentences.

MEETING INDIVIDUAL NEEDS

Phonics: Short a

Write the vocabulary words *sand* and *catch* on the board.

- Emphasize the short *a* sound in each word as you say it. Have children repeat the words.
- Ask a volunteer to draw a circle around the letter that makes the short *a* sound in each word.
- Reread "Fun in the Sand" and ask children to raise their hands when they hear the other word that has the short *a* sound. Write the word on the board. *(castle)*

- Have children brainstorm other words that have short *a*. Suggest that they think of words that rhyme with some of the words on the board.

You may want to refer to pages 79–90 in *MCP Phonics*, Level A for additional practice with short *a*.

You can use the following *MCP Ready Readers*, Stage 1, Book 1, Stage 2, Books 1, 6, 8, 10, 12, 13, 43

ESL Strategy

Model the direction words *circle*, *fill in*, and *underline* and ask children to repeat your actions while saying the words.

Multiple Intelligences: Bodily-Kinesthetic

Play Simon Says. Remind children to listen carefully to the directions and to follow only the directions that begin with "Simon says . . ."

Home-School Connection

Suggest that children and a family member do a household chore together, such as set the table, sort laundry, or feed the cat. While completing the task, they can take turns giving and following simple directions.

LESSON 2 Using Details (pages 9–12)

Objective: Children can identify details in pictures and sentences.

Teaching TIPS

- Identifying details will enrich children's understanding of what they read and see.
- Recalling details will help make the reading and visual experience longer lasting.

Skills Reviewed and Maintained

Comprehension
Picture Clues   See Teach
Making Predictions   See Reading Passage 2

Phonics
Short *u*   See Practicing Vocabulary, Phonics Mini-Lesson

Writing
Sentences   See Making the Reading and Writing Connection

Teach

Display an animal picture, preferably one in which the animal is doing something.

- Put a chart like the following on the board. Write the name of the animal at the top of the chart. Ask children to look closely at the picture and describe what they see. Write their observations under the animal's name.

Tiger
has many stripes
has orange and black fur
has a long tail

STRATEGY: Using Details • Lesson 2   T39

- Tell children that pictures can sometimes tell a story. Invite volunteers to use the picture and the details in the chart to tell a story of their own.
- Next, have children describe what they see in the picture of the bear on page 9. Prompt them with questions such as, "What is happening in this picture?" and "Where does the bear live?"
- Explain that these picture clues will help them answer the questions on the page.
- Read each question and have children indicate the correct picture. As children complete the exercise, check for understanding.

Practice

Introducing Vocabulary

Before children read the sentences, introduce the vocabulary words *(nuts, bears, cubs, fish)* and discuss their meanings. Display a picture of each word. Have volunteers refer to the pictures as they use the words in oral sentences.

Practicing Comprehension Skills

Reading Passage 1

Have children describe what they see in the pictures on page 10. Ask them to name the details in the pictures that help them decide which answer to choose for each exercise.

Reading Passage 2

- Direct children to read the title of the article on page 11. Ask them to look at the picture and make predictions about what they think "Time to Eat" will be about.
- Have children look at the picture and then read the article about what bears like to eat.
- Direct children to complete the exercises on pages 11 and 12. Then review the answers with them.

Practicing Vocabulary

Have children identify the two words that have the short *u* sound. *(nuts, cubs)* Then direct children to complete the vocabulary exercises independently. Review the answers with the class.

Apply

Making the Reading and Writing Connection

Have volunteers share their animal drawings and sentences with the class. Ask classmates to describe what they see in the pictures. Then have them discuss how each picture and sentence go together.

You may want to refer to The Write Direction *Grade 1 for additional opportunities in writing sentences.*

MEETING INDIVIDUAL NEEDS

Phonics: Short *u*

Write *nuts* and *cubs* on the board.

- Say each word, emphasizing the short *u* sound. Have children repeat the words.
- Tell children that these words have the short *u* sound.
- Ask children to clap their hands when you say a word that has the short *u* sound. Say: *cup, bug, dance, gum, tree, duck.*

You may want to refer to pages 107–116 in MCP Phonics, *Level A for additional practice with short* u.

You may want to use the following MCP Ready Readers, *Stage 2, Books 5, 7, 8, 14, 15, 47, Stage 3, Books 12, 13, 23–26, 37.*

ESL Strategy

Children acquiring English can work together to identify other details in the lesson pictures. Help them create a picture dictionary using photos from old magazines. Have the more proficient English speaker write the words.

Multiple Intelligences: Verbal-Linguistic, Interpersonal

Have children work with a partner to look through magazines or newspapers to find a picture they like. Then have them write words to describe the picture. Invite them to share their words and pictures with the class.

Home-School Connection

Suggest to children that they look through a family photograph album and describe the pictures to a family member.

Lesson 2 • STRATEGY: Using Details

Main Idea (pages 13–16)

Objective: Children can identify the main idea in a group of sentences.

Teaching TIPS

- Children remember what they read when they identify the main idea.
- Children determine the importance of what they read when they identify the main idea.

Skills Reviewed and Maintained

Comprehension
Using Details — See Teach, See Reading Passage 1
Predicting — See Reading Passage 2
Following Directions — See Reading Passage 2

Phonics
y as a vowel — See Practicing Vocabulary, Phonics Mini-Lesson

Writing
A Sentence — See Making the Reading and Writing Connection

Teach

Display a picture for children. Invite volunteers to describe the picture. Model how to identify the main idea by asking, "What is the picture all about?" Explain that the "main idea" tells what a picture or story is all about.

- Direct children to the pictures on page 13. Tell them to follow along as you read the sentences to the right of each picture.
- Have children draw a line under the sentence that tells the main idea of each picture. Check for understanding by asking children to explain their choices.

Practice

Introducing Vocabulary

Before children read the story, introduce the vocabulary words *(sky, another, bird, fly)* and discuss their meanings. Together with children use the Glossary to find the definitions of the words. Suggest that children create oral sentences with each word.

Practicing Comprehension Skills

Reading Passage 1

- Read the story on page 14 with children. Then invite volunteers to read sentences 1, 2, and 3. Help children identify the sentence that tells the story's main idea.
- Explain that the other sentences are details (or small pieces of information) that tell more about the main idea.
- Direct children to complete exercises 1–4. Ask children to choose the best name for the story. Discuss the reasons for their choice.

Reading Passage 2

- Direct children to the poem on page 15. Ask them to look at the picture and predict what the poem will be about.
- Have children read the poem and discuss the main idea.
- Invite children to complete the activities on pages 15–16. Then review the answers with them.

Practicing Vocabulary

- Review the vocabulary words with children. Have them identify the two words that have the long *i* sound. *(sky, fly)*
- Direct children to complete the vocabulary exercise independently. Go over the answers with the group.

Apply

Making the Reading and Writing Connection

Invite volunteers to read their main idea sentence and title. The class can predict what each corresponding picture will look like.

You may want to refer to *The Write Direction* Grade 1 for additional opportunities in writing sentences.

STRATEGY: Identifying the Main Idea • **Lesson 3**   T41

MEETING INDIVIDUAL NEEDS

Phonics: y as a Vowel
Write the vocabulary words *sky* and *fly* on the chalkboard.

- Say each word, emphasizing the long *i* sound.
- Underline the letter *y*. Explain that the *y* has a long *i* sound when it is at the end of a word as in the words *sky* and *fly*.
- Reread the poem on page 15 and have children listen for words with the long *i* sound at the end (*butterfly, by, sky, fly*)
- Encourage children to suggest other words with a long *i* sound at the end. When they suggest one that ends in *y* (*cry, my, why, fry*), write the word on the board and underline the *y*.

You may want to refer to pages 259–260 in *MCP Phonics*, Level A for additional practice with *y* as a vowel.

You may want to use the following *MCP Ready Readers*, Stage 4, Books 10–13 for more practice with *y* as a vowel.

ESL Strategy
Children acquiring English can work together to draw a picture that shows what the story on page 14 is about. Have children share their drawings as they identify the story's main idea.

Multiple Intelligences: Verbal-Linguistic
Ask children to think of a familiar story they would like to retell—for example, *The Little Red Hen*. Have volunteers introduce the story by telling the class what it is about. (For example, "This story is about a little red hen that asked her friends to help her bake bread.")

Home-School Connection
Suggest that children watch a television show with a family member. When the show is over, they can work together to identify its main idea.

LESSON 4: Main Idea and Details (pages 17–20)

Objective: Children can identify the main idea and details in an article.

Teaching TIPS
- Children gain a better understanding of the relative importance of the information they read.
- Children recognize that identifying details helps them understand what they read.

Skills Reviewed and Maintained

Comprehension
Drawing Conclusions — See Reading Passage 1
Realism and Fantasy — See Reading Passage 1

Phonics
l Blends: *pl, bl* — See Practicing Vocabulary, Phonics Mini-Lesson

Writing
Sentences — See Making the Reading and Writing Connection

Teach
Help children create sentences about different kinds of ball games.

- Distribute the Graphic Organizer on page T77 of this Guide. Help children think of a sentence that tells the most important thing about their sentences on the board.

Main Idea	There are many kinds of ball games.
Detail	Ping-Pong uses a small white ball.
Detail	Basketball uses a big orange ball.
Detail	A soccer ball is black and white.

- Together, fill in the main idea on the graphic organizer. Then write the details from the board in the Detail spaces.
- Review the picture and then read the story on page 17 together.

Lesson 4 • STRATEGY: Main Idea and Details

- As children complete the exercises, suggest that they look at the story and the picture to help them choose an answer.
- Check for understanding by asking children to explain their answers.

Practice

Introducing Vocabulary
Before children read the sentences, introduce the vocabulary words *(balloon, blimp, pilot, plane)* and discuss their meanings. Have children use the words in sentences of their own.

Practicing Comprehension Skills

Reading Passage 1
- Discuss with children what the picture on page 18 shows. Then have them predict what the article will be about. Remind them to look for details as they read to help them identify the main idea.
- After completing the exercises, ask children questions to help them draw conclusions about being a pilot. For example: Do you think being a pilot is easy or hard? Would you like to be a pilot? Why or why not?
- Talk about whether the information in this passage is real or make-believe.

Reading Passage 2
- Direct children to the article on page 19. Have them look at the picture and predict what the article will be about.
- After children read the article, invite them to discuss what they learned about blimps.
- As children complete the exercises, encourage them to identify details in the article that helped them answer the questions.

Practicing Vocabulary
- Have children identify the two words that begin with an *l* blend. *(blimp, plane)*
- Direct children to complete the vocabulary exercise independently. Review the answers with the group.

Apply

Making the Reading and Writing Connection
Ask volunteers to show their pictures and read their sentences aloud. Have children suggest a name for each picture and sentence.

You may want to refer to *The Write Direction* Grade 1 for additional opportunities in writing sentences.

MEETING INDIVIDUAL NEEDS

Phonics: *l* Blends: *pl, bl*
Write the blends *pl* and *bl* at the top of two columns on the chalkboard. Say the sound of each blend as you run your finger under the letters. Have children repeat the sounds.

- Say the word *plane* and have children repeat it. Ask which column has the same beginning sound as *plane*. Write *plane* under *pl*. Repeat with the word *blimp*.
- Ask children to listen carefully as you say these words: *black, plate, block, please, play, blue*. Call on volunteers to write each word under the appropriate column on the board.

You may want to refer to pages 245–248 in *MCP Phonics*, Level A for additional practice with *l* blends *pl* and *bl*.

You may want to use the following *MCP Ready Readers*, Stage 2, Books 26, 27, for more practice with *l* blends *pl* and *bl*.

ESL Strategy
Suggest a main idea sentence such as *The boys and girls are having fun.* or *The animals are busy.* Help children find magazine or storybook pictures that depict the main idea.

Multiple Intelligences: Visual-Spatial, Verbal-Linguistic
Have children draw or cut out pictures of different types of transportation and make a group poster or bulletin board display. Then help them come up with a title for their pictures.

Home-School Connection
Suggest that children read a story with a family member and then tell the story's main idea.

STRATEGY: Main Idea and Details • Lesson 4 T43

LESSON 5: Summarizing (pages 21–24)

Objective: Children can identify what is important in a story or article.

Teaching TIP

- Children organize information and evaluate the importance of what they have read when they summarize.

Skills Reviewed and Maintained

Comprehension
Main Idea and Details — See Teach, Reading Passage 1
Making Predictions — See Reading Passage 1, Reading Passage 2

Phonics
Digraph *sh* — See Practicing Vocabulary, Phonics Mini-Lesson

Writing
Summary Sentences — See Making the Reading and Writing Connection

Teach

Help children write a class story with the title "Our Jobs at Home."

- Draw an eight-panel storyboard on the board.
- Have volunteers draw an event of the story on each panel.
- Have other volunteers label each event.
- Display the Graphic Organizer on page T75 of this Guide. Ask children to look at the class story they have written on the storyboard and pick out the important ideas. Write their responses in the first two rectangles.

> We feed our pets.
> We clear the table.

> We walk our dogs.
> We take out the trash.

- Then help children summarize their story using only one sentence.

> We do many jobs to help at home.

- Read page 21 together. Have children choose the sentence that tells about the important parts of the sentences on this page. Ask them to explain their answer.

On Your Own Practice

Introducing Vocabulary

Before children read the story, introduce the vocabulary words (*different, shade, shoes, warm*) and discuss their meanings. Together as a class, use the Glossary to find the definitions of the words. Have children work with partners to create oral short stories using the words. Have other children summarize the short stories.

Practicing Comprehension Skills

Reading Passage 1

- Discuss with children what the pictures on page 22 show. Then have them predict what the article will be about. Remind them to look for important parts of the article as they read.
- Model finding the main idea and the important parts of the article by asking, "What are these sentences about?" Then ask children to help you decide what information is important or what is not important as they complete the exercises.
- Encourage children to identify details in the story that helped them answer question 3.

Reading Passage 2

- Direct children to the article on page 23. Have them look at the pictures and predict what "Working Shoes" will be about.
- After reading, discuss which parts of the article are important and which parts are not. Then have children complete the exercises.

Practicing Vocabulary

- Have children identify the two words that begin with the digraph *sh*. (*shade, shoes*)
- Direct children to complete the vocabulary exercise independently. Review the answers with the group.

T44 Lesson 5 • STRATEGY: Summarizing

Apply

Making the Reading and Writing Connection

Have volunteers show their pictures to the class. Ask children to tell what each picture is about. Then have the volunteer read his or her sentence about the picture.

You may want to refer to *The Write Direction* Grade 1 for additional opportunities in writing sentences.

MEETING INDIVIDUAL NEEDS

Phonics: Digraph *sh*

Model making the "be quiet" sound by putting your finger to your lips and saying "shhh." Have children do the same.

- Write the vocabulary words *shoes* and *shade* on the chalkboard. Say each word, emphasizing the digraph *sh*. Have children repeat the words. Circle the *sh* in each word.

- Ask children to think of other words that begin like *shoes* and *shade*. Call on volunteers to write the words on the board and circle the letters that represent the *sh* sound. Words might include *shop, shorts, she, shout,* and *show*.

You may want to refer to pages 279–280 in *MCP Phonics*, Level A for additional practice with the digraph *sh*.

You may want to use the following *MCP Ready Readers*, Stage 0, Book 42, Stage 0/1, Book 48, Stage 2, Books, 31, 32, for more practice with the digraph *sh*.

ESL Strategy

Have children draw a picture of shoes they like, and then describe them to a partner. Children can work together to write a sentence that tells the most important thing about the shoes.

Multiple Intelligences: Verbal-Linguistic, Interpersonal

Have children work in small groups. Each child selects a favorite storybook from the classroom library and shows it to the others. Then he or she tells the most important parts of the story. Suggest that children may want to use pictures in the book to help them retell the story.

Home-School Connection

Suggest that children read a book or watch a television show with a family member. Afterward, children can retell the story in their own words.

Lesson 6: Drawing Conclusions (pages 25–28)

Objective: Children can use picture and word clues to draw conclusions.

Teaching TIPS

- Children recognize that drawing conclusions from what they read makes reading more interesting.
- Children realize that drawing conclusions from pictures and words is an important strategy to use as they read.

Skills Reviewed and Maintained

Comprehension
Main Idea and Details   See Reading Passage 1
Picture Clues   See Reading Passage 2

Phonics
Short *i*   See Practicing Vocabulary, Phonics Mini-Lesson

Writing
Clues   See Making the Reading and Writing Connection

Teach

Away from the rest of the class, ask three volunteers to use their faces and bodies to act happy, sad, and tired.

- After volunteers perform, ask the class to tell how each child felt.

- Discuss with children how they were able to tell how each performer felt. Guide them to conclude that each performer's actions, such as facial expressions, were clues.

STRATEGY: Drawing Conclusions • Lesson 6   T45

- Point out to children that they can look for clues in the pictures and words they read to help them understand what is happening in a story.
- Review each picture and then read the sentences on page 25 together. What clues helped them to select the right sentence?
- As children complete the exercise, suggest that they look for clues in the picture that would help them choose the right sentence.

Practice

Introducing Vocabulary
Before children read the story, introduce the vocabulary words (*sleep, quit, smell, pick*) and discuss their meanings. Ask questions that require children to use the words in their answers. For example, *What do you do during nap time?*

Practicing Comprehension Skills

Reading Passage 1
- Discuss with children what the picture on page 26 shows. Then have them predict what the story will be about. Remind them to look for clues in the picture and words as they read.
- After they read the story, ask children to tell the main idea. Discuss the important information that helps them tell what the story is about. Then have them complete the exercises.

Reading Passage 2
- Direct children to the story on page 27. Have them read the title and look at the picture to predict what "Bill Tries to Sleep" will be about.
- Have children read the story. Discuss picture clues that help them understand what is happening in the story.
- Direct children to complete the exercises on pages 27 and 28. Encourage children to identify the clues they used to answer each question.

Practicing Vocabulary
- Have children identify the two words that have the short *i* sound. (*pick, quit*)
- Direct children to complete the vocabulary exercise independently. Review the answers with the group.

Apply

Making the Reading and Writing Connection
Have partners read their clues to each other and guess each other's food pictures. Encourage them to discuss other clues that could have been used.

MEETING INDIVIDUAL NEEDS

Phonics: Short *i*
Write the vocabulary words *pick* and *quit* on the chalkboard.

- Emphasize the short *i* sound as you say each word. Have children repeat the words.
- Ask a volunteer to draw a circle around the letter that makes the short *i* sound in each word.
- Reread both passages in this lesson and ask children to raise their hands each time they hear a word with short *i*. List the words on the board. (*Kim, visit, pick, Bill, is, pig, singing, window*)

You may want to refer to pages 93–102 in *MCP Phonics,* Level A for additional practice with short *i*.

You may want to use the following *MCP Ready Readers,* Stage 2, Books 2, 6, 16, 44, Stage 3, Books 4–6, 16, 17, 34, Stage 4, Books 7, 12–14.

ESL Strategy
Show children pictures from classroom books and ask them to work with partners to tell how the people are feeling or what they think will happen next. Help them create lists of words on chart paper and encourage them to illustrate the words and use them as reference for future activities.

Multiple Intelligences: Naturalist
Have children think about clues they might find outdoors that would tell them that an animal has been nearby, such as feathers, nests, or footprints. Suggest that they draw pictures that their classmates can use to guess what kind of animal it is.

Home-School Connection
Suggest that children and family members play a game of charades. They can take turns acting out different jobs done around the house and guessing what each person is doing.

 Lesson 6 • STRATEGY: Drawing Conclusions

LESSON 7: Drawing Conclusions (pages 29–32)

Objective: Children can use picture and word clues to draw conclusions.

Teaching TIPS

- Children synthesize and evaluate information by drawing conclusions.
- Children bring their own life experiences to what they read by drawing conclusions.

Skills Reviewed and Maintained

Comprehension
Cause and Effect — See Reading Passage 1
Main Idea and Details — See Reading Passage 2

Phonics
Long *u* — See Practicing Vocabulary, Phonics Mini-Lesson

Writing
Riddles — See Making the Reading and Writing Connection

Teach

Tell children to pretend they are detectives. They should listen to the clues you are going to give them to figure out the answer to this riddle about a school worker.

> I work all around the school.
> I keep the school clean.
> I fix things that are broken.
> Who am I?

- Name some school workers, such as nurse, librarian, teacher, custodian, cafeteria worker. Ask children if they have seen any of these workers do the jobs mentioned in the riddle. Lead children to recognize that the school custodian performs all these jobs.
- Point out to children that they should look for word and picture clues when they read to help them understand what is happening. Then direct them to read the riddles on page 29.
- As children complete the exercises, encourage them to look for clues in the pictures to help them decide which words to underline.
- Check for understanding by having children describe the clues they used.

Practice

Introducing Vocabulary

Before children read the riddles, introduce the vocabulary words *(use, ring, huge, letters)* and discuss their meanings. You may want to make up a fill-in-the-blank sentence for each vocabulary word and have children supply the missing word.

Practicing Comprehension Skills

Reading Passage 1

- Review each of the pictures on page 30 with children and have them describe what each person is doing. Then have them complete the activity.
- Provide children an opportunity to practice recognizing cause-and-effect relationships by asking questions about each riddle, such as, "Why does the mail carrier have a huge bag?" or "How does a doctor make sick people feel better?"

Reading Passage 2

- Direct children to read the title of the story on page 31 and tell what they think "The Missing Ring" will be about.
- Discuss how word and picture clues can help children understand what is happening in the story. Have children identify the main idea of this story.
- Direct children to complete the exercises on pages 31 and 32. Encourage them to identify the clues they used to answer each question.

Practicing Vocabulary

- Ask children which vocabulary words have the long *u* sound. *(huge, use)*
- Direct children to complete the vocabulary exercise independently, and then review the answers as a group.

STRATEGY: Drawing Conclusions • Lesson 7 T47

Apply

Making the Reading and Writing Connection

Have partners share their riddles. Encourage them to tell which clues helped them solve each other's riddle.

You may want to refer to *The Write Direction* Grade 1 for additional opportunities in writing riddles.

MEETING INDIVIDUAL NEEDS

Phonics: Long *u*

Write *use* and *huge* on the chalkboard.

- Emphasize the long *u* sound as you say each word. Have children repeat the words.
- Tell children that these words have the same long *u* sound that they hear in the word *ruler*.
- Say this sentence, inserting a new final word each time: *Look at that huge _____* (mule, house, cube, dune, book, tube). Tell children to raise their hands if the last word in the sentence has the long *u* sound.

You may want to refer to pages 183–192 in *MCP Phonics*, Level A for additional practice with long *u*.

You may want to use the following *MCP Ready Readers*, Stage 2, Book 47, Stage 3, Books 12, 13, 23–26, 37, for more practice with long *u*.

ESL Strategy

Have children describe what each person in the pictures on page 30 is doing. Then help them make up riddles of their own to go with each picture.

Multiple Intelligences: Visual-Spatial, Verbal-Linguistic

Display interesting pictures of people and animals from magazines and newspapers. Ask children to look for clues in the pictures that they can use to tell what is happening. Invite children to share experiences they have had that relate to the pictures.

Home-School Connection

Suggest that children and a family member have a treasure hunt, where one person hides something and then gives clues to help the other person find the "treasure."

LESSON 8: Sequence of Events (pages 33–36)

Objective: Children can identify the order of events in a story.

Teaching TIPS

- Identifying the order of events in a story helps children develop an awareness of time relationships.
- Identifying the order of events in a story helps children acquire other comprehension skills that require organized and logical thinking.

Skills Reviewed and Maintained

Comprehension
Following Directions   See Reading Passage 1
Main Idea and Details   See Reading Passage 2

Phonics
Long *e*   See Practicing Vocabulary, Phonics Mini-Lesson

Writing
Story   See Making the Reading and Writing Connection

Teach

Draw three pictures on the board: a seed, a seedling, a full-grown plant.

- Call on volunteers to number the pictures 1, 2, and 3 to tell what happens first, what happens next, and what happens last.
- Point out to children that they should think about the order in which things happen when they read a story. They should think about what happens first, next, and last.
- Have children look at the first three pictures on page 33. Ask them to describe what happens first, next, and last.

- As children complete the exercise, remind them to think about the order in which things happen.
- Check for understanding by having children explain how they decided what happened first, next, and last.

 **Practice**

Introducing Vocabulary
Before children read the story, introduce the vocabulary words *(dream, kitchen, reads, school)* and discuss their meanings. You may want to suggest that children use the Glossary to find the definition for each word.

Practicing Comprehension Skills
Reading Passage 1
- Have children read the title of the story on page 34 and discuss what the pictures show. Then have them predict what the story will be about. Remind them to look for clues in the pictures and words that tell the order in which things happen.
- After reading, ask children what words in the story are clues to the order in which things happen. Give students an opportunity to practice following directions by having them circle these clue words. Point out that these are the same words they are going to put under the pictures.

Reading Passage 2
- Direct children to the story on page 35. Have them look at the picture and the title and predict who the friends are in "A Buzzy Day."
- As children read the story, encourage them to identify words that help them figure out the order in which things happen.
- After reading, have children identify the main idea in this story.
- Direct children to complete the exercises on pages 35 and 36. When they finish, discuss how they decided to order the events in the story.

Practicing Vocabulary
- Have children identify the two words that have the long *e* sound. *(dream, reads)*
- Read the directions and have children complete the vocabulary exercise independently. Review the answers together.

Apply
Making the Reading and Writing Connection
Ask volunteers to share their robot pictures and sentences with the class. Call on children at random to tell what happened first, next, or last as they look at the pictures.

You may want to refer to *The Write Direction* Grade 1 for additional opportunities in writing stories.

MEETING INDIVIDUAL NEEDS

Phonics: Long *e*
Draw attention to the two vocabulary words that have the long *e* sound: *dream, reads*. Say the words aloud and have children repeat them.

- Write the words on the board and circle the letters *ea*. Explain that the letters *ea* can make the long *e* sound that they hear in *dream* and *reads*.
- Have children listen for other words that have the long *e* sound as you reread "Dee and Robo" and "A Buzzy Day." *(Dee, eats, sleep)* Point out that the letters *ee* can also make the long *e* sound.

You may want to refer to pages 217–226 in *MCP Phonics*, Level A for additional practice with long *e*.

You may want to use the following *MCP Ready Readers*, Stage 2, Book 46, Stage 3, Books 10, 11, 20–22, for more practice with long *e*.

ESL Strategy
Children can role-play the actions of the characters in the stories and hold up number cards to show the order in which the actions happened.

Multiple Intelligences: Musical, Interpersonal
Put children in groups of four. Have each group tell a round-robin story. Each person can add a part to the story. One child begins the story with the word *first*. Others add to the story using the words *then, next*, and *last*.

Home-School Connection
Suggest that children talk with a family member about what they did during the day. As they talk, they can use words such as *first, next, then,* and *last* to tell the order in which things happened.

STRATEGY: Identifying Sequence of Events • **Lesson 8**

LESSON 9: Sequence of Events (pages 37–40)

Objective: Children can identify the order of events in a story.

Teaching TIPS

- Recognizing the sequence of events in a story is an important strategy for thinking logically when reading.
- Understanding the sequence of events in a story promotes comprehension.

Skills Reviewed and Maintained

Comprehension
Making Predictions — See Introducing Vocabulary
Drawing Conclusions — See Reading Passage 2

Phonics
Long a — See Practicing Vocabulary, Phonics Mini-Lesson

Writing
Sequence Story — See Making the Reading and Writing Connection

Teach

Dramatize three activities people do when they wake up, such as stretching, brushing their teeth, washing hands and face, and eating breakfast.

- Ask children to tell what you did first, next, and last. Talk about why people do things in a certain order as they get ready in the morning.
- Write this chart on the board and help children fill it in with sentences that tell the order they follow in playing a familiar game.

First
Next
Last

- Point out to children that the order in which things happen is as important as the things themselves. Explain that clue words like *first, next, then,* and *last* help them keep track of order. Then direct them to look at the pictures on page 37.
- Encourage children to look at the details in the pictures as they think about the story the pictures tell. Discuss what happens first, next, and last.
- Check for understanding by reviewing children's responses to the exercises.

On Your Own Practice

Introducing Vocabulary

Before children read the story, introduce the vocabulary words *(made, cake, first, plates)* and discuss their meanings. Encourage children to use the words to predict what they will read about next.

Practicing Comprehension Skills

Reading Passage 1

- Direct children to read the title of the story on page 38 and then look at the picture. Ask them to predict what "A Special Day" will be about.
- As they read the story, remind children to look for clue words that tell about the order in which things happen.
- Help children conclude that Jane covered the cake and wanted her dad to close his eyes because she was planning a surprise.

Reading Passage 2

- Read "Sam's Surprise" together. Then ask children to identify the clue words that help them figure out the order in which things happen. *(first, next, then, at last)* Review why it is important to pay attention to clue words as they read.
- Encourage children to refer to the story as they complete the activity on page 39. When children finish, review and discuss their answers.

Practicing Vocabulary

Have children identify the words that have the long *a* sound. *(made, cake, plates)* Direct children to complete the exercise on their own. Then review the answers with the group.

T50 Lesson 9 • STRATEGY: Identifying Sequence of Events

Apply

Making the Reading and Writing Connection

Call on volunteers to share their pictures and read their stories. Have classmates identify the words in each story that tell the order in which things happen.

You may want to refer to *The Write Direction* Grade 1 for additional opportunities in writing a sequence story.

MEETING INDIVIDUAL NEEDS

Phonics: Long *a*

Write the vocabulary words *made*, *cake*, and *plates* on the board.

- Emphasize the long *a* sound as you say each word. Ask children to repeat the words.

- Give each child a paper plate. Direct them to write other words that have the long *a* sound on their plates. Suggest they think of rhyming words for the vocabulary words on the board.

- Have a long *a* party where children share the words that are on their plates.

You may want to refer to pages 153–166 in *MCP Phonics*, Level A for additional practice with long *a*.

You may want to use the following *MCP Ready Readers*, Stage 2, Book 43, Stage 3, Books 1–3, 14, 15, 33 for more practice with long *a*.

ESL Strategy

Have children draw three pictures to show the steps in a familiar process, such as brushing teeth or making chocolate milk. Then have them make three cards with the labels *first*, *next*, and *last*. Have children work together to put the pictures in order, matching each picture with its correct label.

Multiple Intelligences: Verbal-Linguistic, Visual-Spatial

Have each child draw a picture showing something the class did today: reading a story, planting seeds, and so on. Display the pictures and work with the class to put them in order, using such words as *first*, *next*, *then*, and *last*.

Home-School Connection

Suggest that children recall a birthday or other family celebration and tell a family member about it, using clue words to show the order in which things happened.

LESSON 10 Predicting Outcomes (pages 41–44)

Objective: Children can use picture and word clues to make predictions.

Teaching TIPS

- Making predictions helps children understand the logical progression of what they read.
- Making predictions helps children identify with the action and characters in a story.

Skills Reviewed and Maintained

Comprehension
Main Idea and Details   See Reading Passage 1
Sequence of Events   See Reading Passage 2

Phonics
sn, sl   See Practicing Vocabulary, Phonics Mini-Lesson

Writing
Story Starter   See Making the Reading and Writing Connection

Teach

- Explain to children that sometimes you can tell what is going to happen next by looking at what is happening now.

- Present some simple "predicting riddles," such as those below. Encourage children to identify the clues that lead them to their answers.

It is a breezy day.   The family is on a picnic.
Mark takes out his kite.   The sky gets very dark.
What will Mark do next?   What happens next?

STRATEGY: Predicting Outcomes • Lesson 10   T51

- Tell children that when they read, they should look for clues in the words and pictures to help them tell what will happen next. Then direct them to the first exercise on page 41.
- Suggest to children that they think about what they would do if the story were about them.
- As children complete the exercises, check for understanding by observing the clues they identify and talk about.

Practice

Introducing Vocabulary
Before children read the story, introduce the vocabulary words *(again, snow, help, sled)* and discuss their meanings. Ask children to use the words in sentences about a winter day.

Practicing Comprehension Skills
Reading Passage 1
- Before children begin the exercise on page 42, remind them to look for clues in the words and pictures that will help them decide what happens next. You may wish to work through the first activity with children, and then have them complete the rest of the exercises on their own.
- Review the main idea by asking children to identify which of the following sentences tells what the first story is mostly about: *Sam goes sledding. Sam makes a sled.*
- Discuss with children the details in the story and pictures that helped them choose an answer.

Reading Passage 2
- Have children discuss the illustration at the top of page 43 and predict what they think "Frosty Friends" will be about.
- After children read the story, review the sequence of events by having them identify what happened first, next, and last. Then ask children what they think will happen next.
- After children complete the exercises on pages 43 and 44, discuss the answers together.

Practicing Vocabulary
- Ask children to identify the vocabulary words that begin with *sn* and *sl*. *(snowy, sled)*

- Children can complete the exercise on their own. Then review the answers with the group.

Apply
Making the Reading and Writing Connection
Have partners share their story starters and endings with the class. Invite children to suggest other ways the stories could end.

You may want to refer to *The Write Direction* Grade 1 for additional opportunities in writing a story starter.

MEETING INDIVIDUAL NEEDS

Phonics: *sn, sl*
Write the vocabulary words *snow* and *sled* on the board.
- Say each word aloud, emphasizing the initial /sn/ and /sl/ sounds. Have children repeat the words as you circle the letters *sn* and *sl*.
- Ask children to listen as you say these words: *snack, slice, slim, snail, sneak, slow, slush, snore, snip*. After each word, have children tell whether the word has the same beginning sound as *snow* or *sled*. Then write the word under the appropriate vocabulary word on the board.

You may want to refer to pages 249–252 in *MCP Phonics*, Level A for additional practice with the blend *sn*.

You may want to use the following *MCP Ready Readers*, Stage 0, Book 42, Stage 2, Books 32, 33, for more practice with *sn*.

ESL Strategy
Show children magazine pictures of common occurrences, such as a family in a car, a baseball player at bat, or a cloudy sky. After talking about each picture, ask children to tell what might happen next.

Multiple Intelligences: Verbal-Linguistic, Interpersonal
Have partners read up to a marked page in a book, then draw a picture of what they think will happen next. Suggest they confirm or revise their prediction by finishing the book.

Home-School Connection
Suggest that children and a family member read a story together, stopping several times to predict what will happen next.

T52 Lesson 10 • STRATEGY: Predicting Outcomes

Predicting Outcomes (pages 45–48)

Objective: Children can use text clues and prior knowledge to make predictions.

Teaching TIPS

- Children become more engaged in the outcome of a story or article when they make predictions.
- Children realize that prior knowledge can help them understand what they are reading.

Skills Reviewed and Maintained

Comprehension
Visualizing   See Teach
Using Details   See Reading Passage 1

Phonics
Consonant Digraph *wh*   See Practicing Vocabulary, Phonics Mini-Lesson

Writing
Story   See Making the Reading and Writing Connection

Teach

Ask children to close their eyes and visualize what is happening in this story as you read it aloud.

> Jake finished putting his animal drawings into a neat pile. He set them on a table near an open window. Suddenly, the wind blew very hard.

- Distribute the Graphic Organizer on page T76 of this Guide.

| What I predict will happen | What did happen |

- Ask children to tell what they think will happen next in the story. Suggest that they think about what happens to things when the wind is blowing. Have them record their predictions in the graphic organizer.
- Read the rest of the story:

> The papers blew all over the room. Jake closed the window and picked them up.

- Ask children to tell what really happened and record their responses on the right side of their chart. Help them decide if the ending matched what they thought would happen next.

- Tell children that when they read, they should think about what they already know and look for clues in the pictures and words to help them tell what will happen next. Then direct children to complete the activity on page 45 and talk about how they arrived at their answers.

 **Practice**

Introducing Vocabulary

Before children read the story, introduce the vocabulary words (*whale, captain, why, raincoats*) and discuss their meanings. Call on volunteers to look up the meaning of each word in the Glossary and share it with the class.

Practicing Comprehension Skills

Reading Passage 1

- Have children read the story title and look at the picture on page 46. Encourage them to identify details in the picture and share what they know about whales. Then help them use this information to predict what "Whale Watch" will be about.
- Before children begin the activities, remind them to look for clues in the picture and words, and use what they already know, to answer the questions. Review and discuss children's responses.

Reading Passage 2

- Have children look at the picture and read the story title on page 47. Ask them to predict who will be "wet like whales."
- After children read the story, discuss what they think happens next. Then have them complete the exercise.
- Review each of the questions and answer choices. Call on volunteers to explain their decisions.

Practicing Vocabulary

Ask children to identify the two vocabulary words that begin with the *wh* sound. (*whale, why*) After children complete the vocabulary exercise, review their answers.

STRATEGY: Predicting Outcomes • Lesson 11

T53

Apply

Making the Reading and Writing Connection

After children read their stories, call on volunteers to tell how they made predictions about the stories' endings. What story clues did they use? What did they already know about the animals that helped them?

You may want to refer to *The Write Direction* Grade 1 for additional opportunities in writing a story.

MEETING INDIVIDUAL NEEDS

Phonics: Consonant Digraph *wh*

Write the vocabulary words *whale* and *why* on the board.

- Ask children to echo the sound *wh* represents as you pronounce each word.
- Point out that children hear this sound at the beginning of other question words, such as *what, when,* and *where.*
- Have children ask questions about whales using *wh* words, for example, "What do whales eat?" and "Where do whales live?" Have volunteers find answers to the questions and report back to class.

You may want to refer to pages 277–278 in *MCP Phonics,* Level A for additional practice with consonant digraph *wh*.

You may want to use the following *MCP Ready Readers,* Stage 0, Book 46, Stage 0/1, Book 50, Stage 2, Book 36, for more practice with consonant digraph *wh*.

ESL Strategy

Read a short story to children and stop at a designated point. Have children draw pictures to show what they think will happen next.

Multiple Intelligences: Bodily/Kinesthetic

Children can role-play the whales from both of the stories and predict what the whales would say about the people watching them.

Home-School Connection

Suggest that children look at newspaper pictures with a family member and make predictions about what happened right after each picture was taken.

LESSON 12 Cause and Effect (pages 49–52)

Objective: Children can recognize cause-and-effect relationships.

Teaching TIPS

- Children gain a better understanding of what they read by recognizing cause-and-effect relationships.
- Children recognize that understanding cause-and-effect relationships is an important reading strategy.

Skills Reviewed and Maintained

Comprehension
Main Idea and Details   See Reading Passage 1
Making Predictions   See Reading Passage 2

Phonics
l Blend: *fl*   See Practicing Vocabulary, Phonics Mini-Lesson

Writing
Cause and Effect Sentences   See Making the Reading and Writing Connection

Teach

Display an uncovered box that is overfilled with crayons. Work hard to try and put the cover on.

- Then display the Graphic Organizer on page T78 of this Guide. Read the phrase *What happened*. On the lines, write *The crayon box won't close*. Then read the phrase *Why it happened*. Explain that the box won't close because it is too full. Write this reason next to *Why it Happened*.
- Discuss with children that sometimes when one thing happens, it makes something else happen. Encourage

T54   Lesson 12 • STRATEGY: Recognizing Cause-and-Effect Relationships them to offer other examples, and record their ideas on the chart.

1	What happened: The field got muddy.
	Why it happened: It rained last night.
2	What happened: Jed missed the school play.
	Why it happened: He had a bad cold.

- Review the picture story on page 49. Encourage children to picture in their minds what might happen next. Check for understanding.

Practice

Introducing Vocabulary
Before children read the story, introduce the vocabulary words (*flies, flowers, hive, spider*) and discuss their meanings. Then use each word in a question for children to answer, for example, "What are your favorite flowers?"

Practicing Comprehension Skills

Reading Passage 1
- Read the title of the passage and ask children to predict what it will be about. After reading, review main idea by helping children think of one sentence that tells the most important thing about this passage. (*Bees work hard to get food.*)
- Guide children to complete the activity. When they finish, review and discuss their answers. Encourage them to explain how they selected them.

Reading Passage 2
- Read the title with children and discuss the illustration. Then invite them to predict how this story might be alike and different from "A Bee's Life."
- As children read, remind them to think about why things happen. Encourage them to identify how one event causes another event to happen.
- After completing the activity, discuss children's responses. Encourage them to identify words and sentences that helped them select their answers.

Practicing Vocabulary
- Have children identify the two words that begin with the *fl* blend. (*flies, flowers*)

- Have children complete the exercises on their own. Then review the answers with the group.

Apply

Making the Reading and Writing Connection
Call on volunteers to share their pictures and sentences with the class. Encourage children to use the pictures and sentences to state cause-and-effect relationships.

You may want to refer to *The Write Direction* Grade 1 for additional opportunities in writing cause-and-effect sentences.

MEETING INDIVIDUAL NEEDS

Phonics: l Blend: fl
Write the vocabulary words *flies* and *flowers* on the chalkboard.

- Say each word, emphasizing the *fl* sound as you underline the letters. Then have children repeat the words.
- Tell children that you are going to give some directions. They should act out only the directions that contain words that begin with the *fl* sound. Then say: *Smell a flower. Read a book. Fly in place. Wave a flag. Touch the floor.*

You may want to refer to pages 245–248 in *MCP Phonics*, Level A for additional practice with the *fl* blend.

You may want to use the following *MCP Ready Readers*, Stage 2 Book 23, for more practice with the *fl* blend.

ESL Strategy
Children acquiring English may enjoy working together to act out what a bee does to find food. Encourage them to talk about "what happens next."

Multiple Intelligences: Naturalist, Visual-Spatial
Display photos of insects and talk about them in small groups. Have children draw a picture of their favorite bug. Then have them write a sentence that tells something the bug does and why.

Home-School Connection
Suggest that children help a family member prepare a meal. As they work together, they can talk about how one thing makes another thing happen, for example: "*The heat from the stove causes the water to boil.*"

STRATEGY: Recognizing Cause-and-Effect Relationships • Lesson 12

T55

Cause and Effect (pages 53–56)

Objective: Children can recognize cause-and-effect relationships.

Teaching TIPS

- Children gain a better understanding of character motivation by recognizing cause-and-effect relationships.
- Children are able to transfer their understanding of cause-and-effect relationships to other subject areas.

Skills Reviewed and Maintained

Comprehension
Main Idea and Details   See Reading Passage 1
Sequence of Events   See Reading Passage 2

Phonics
r Blends: gr, br   See Practicing Vocabulary, Phonics Mini-Lesson

Writing
Sentences   See Making the Reading and Writing Connection

Teach

Ask children to watch you closely as you mix a few drops of blue and yellow food coloring in a glass of water.

- Have children finish this sentence: The water is green because ____. Ask children to tell what happened to make the water turn green. Remind children that one thing can make another thing happen.
- Distribute the Graphic Organizer on page T78 of this Guide, and help children use it to record some common cause-and-effect relationships.

  1. What happened: I missed Brett's party.
     Why it happened: I was sick.
  2. What happened: I forgot my library book.
     Why it happened: I was late for the bus.

- Explain to children that it helps you understand what you read if you think about the things that happen and why they happen. Then direct them to the activity on page 53.
- Discuss with children what is happening in each picture and why. Then have them complete the exercise.
- Check for understanding by observing the cause and effect relationships that children identify.

 **Practice**

Introducing Vocabulary
Before children begin reading the passages, introduce the vocabulary words (*seed, grow, cook, bring*) and discuss their meanings. You may want to have children use these words in oral sentences about something they have planted or cooked.

Practicing Comprehension Skills

Reading Passage 1

- Read the story aloud as children follow along. Clarify that the main idea of the story is how to grow a bean plant. Then have children identify details that tell how the growing process works.
- Point out the words *so* and *because* in the exercise and ask children which words tell what would happen next in each sentence. Encourage children to discuss why their answers make sense.

Reading Passage 2

- After children read the story title and look at the picture on page 55, ask them to tell what they think the birthday surprise will be.
- Have children read the story independently. Then review sequence of events by asking children to tell what happened first, next, then, and last in the story.
- Direct children to complete the exercises on pages 55 and 56. Remind them to think about what happens and why it happens as they read.

Practicing Vocabulary

- Have children identify the two vocabulary words that begin with an *r* blend. (*bring, grow*)
- Read the directions aloud and have children complete the vocabulary exercise. Then review the answers together.

Lesson 13 • **STRATEGY:** Recognizing Cause-and-Effect Relationships

Apply

Making the Reading and Writing Connection

Ask volunteers to share their before and after pictures and sentences. Then ask children to describe what happened in the pictures using a sentence that includes the word *so* or *because*.

You may wish to refer to *The Write Direction* Grade 1 for additional opportunities in writing cause and effect sentences.

MEETING INDIVIDUAL NEEDS

Phonics: r Blends: *gr, br*

Write the blends *gr* and *br* on the chalkboard. Point to each blend and say its sound.

- Write *grow* under the *gr* heading. Ask a volunteer to circle the letters that make the beginning sound. Emphasize the blend sound as you say the word. Have children say the word after you. Repeat for the word *bring*.

- Brainstorm other words that begin with *gr* and *br*. Write each word under the appropriate heading. Have children read the words aloud. (Possible words: *bread, brain, broken, grape, great, grin*)

You may want to refer to pages 241–244 in *MCP Phonics*, Level A for additional practice with *r* blends.

You may want to use the following *MCP Ready Readers*, Stage 2, Books 28 and 29 and Stage 4, Book 13 for more practice with *r* blends.

ESL Strategy

English-speaking children can dramatize the story events as you reread "A Birthday Surprise." Use the dramatization to review and identify cause-and-effect relationships for children acquiring English.

Multiple Intelligences: Verbal-Linguistic, Interpersonal

Ask partners to continue the story "A Birthday Surprise" by writing about what happens after Dad wakes up. Suggest that they use the words *so* and *because* in their sentences.

Home-School Connection

Suggest that children prepare a meal with a family member and identify causes and effects, such as butter melting because it was heated on the stove.

Lesson 14: Real and Make-Believe (pages 57–60)

Objective: Children can distinguish fantasy from reality.

Teaching TIPS

- Children recognize the difference between a realistic story and one based on fantasy.
- Children use their understanding of realism and fantasy to make the more advanced distinction between nonfiction and fiction.

Skills Reviewed and Maintained

Comprehension
Main Idea and Details   See Reading Passage 1
Drawing Conclusions   See Reading Passage 2

Phonics
Blend *st*   See Practicing Vocabulary, Phonics Mini-Lesson

Writing
Stories   See Making the Reading and Writing Connection

Teach

Ask children if they have ever watched a television show or read a story about something that couldn't really happen. Call on volunteers to share their experiences.

- Write this sentence on the chalkboard: *A cow is sleeping.* Read the sentence aloud and ask children if this could really happen.

- Now write this sentence: *A cow is driving the tractor.* Point out that this could not really happen. It is make-believe because cows cannot really drive.

- Ask children to supply other endings to the sentence starter *A cow. . .* Write each idea on the chalkboard and

STRATEGY: Distinguishing Fantasy from Reality • Lesson 14

ask children to imagine what the cow is doing. Then ask them to think about what they know about cows to decide whether each sentence is real or make-believe.

- Point out to children that some of the stories they read could really happen and some couldn't really happen. Discuss how they can tell the difference. Then direct them to the activities on page 57.

- Encourage children to give reasons for their answers when they respond to questions.

Practice

Introducing Vocabulary
Before children read the passages, introduce the vocabulary words *(star, stay, rockets, kitten)* and discuss their meanings. Use these words in questions that children can answer, such as "Where do rockets go?"

Practicing Comprehension Skills

Reading Passage 1

- Read "Jake's Pets" together. Clarify that the main idea of the story is that Jake has many pet friends. Then ask children to give some details about Jake's pet friends.

- Remind them to think about what is real and what is make-believe. Suggest that they ask themselves, "Could this really happen?" as they read.

- After completing the exercise, encourage children to discuss how they knew what was make-believe and what was real.

Reading Passage 2

- Have children look at the picture and read the title of the story on page 59. Then ask children to tell what they think "Space Race" will be about.

- After completing the activity, review children's responses. Resolve differences by asking, "Could this really happen? Why or why not?"

- Help children conclude that this is a make-believe story since some of its events couldn't really happen.

Practicing Vocabulary

- Have children identify the two words that begin with *st*. *(star, stay)*

- Direct children to complete the vocabulary exercise independently. Review the answers as a group.

Apply

Making the Reading and Writing Connection
Call on volunteers to share their stories. Ask the class to identify which story is real and which story is make-believe. Encourage children to tell how they decided.

You may want to refer to *The Write Direction* Grade 1 for additional opportunities in writing stories.

MEETING INDIVIDUAL NEEDS

Phonics: Blend *st*
Write *star* and *stay* on index cards and read them.

- Ask children to identify the letters that make the beginning sound in each word.

- Have children brainstorm other words that begin with the *st* sound, such as *stair, stamp, stop,* and *storm*. Write each *st* word on an index card.

- Place the word cards in a large pot and tell children they have made an *st* stew. Have volunteers stir the pot of words with a *stirring* spoon. Then have them take a word card from the pot, read it aloud, and use it in a sentence.

You may want to refer to pages 249–252 in *MCP Phonics*, Level A for additional practice with *st* blends.

You may want to use the following *MCP Ready Readers*, Stage 2, Books 23 and 24 for more practice with *st* blends.

ESL Strategy
Show children pictures of real and make-believe objects, such as clothes, space creatures, cartoon characters, and flowers. Ask children to group the pictures into two categories: real and make-believe.

Multiple Intelligences: Bodily-Kinesthetic
Have children make dog and cat masks and role-play the make-believe action in "Space Race." Then suggest that they act out some real things that a cat and dog can do.

Home-School Connection
Children can look through books at home with a family member. Have them use the titles and pictures to decide whether each book is likely to be real or make-believe.

 T58 Lesson 14 • STRATEGY: Distinguishing Fantasy from Reality

LESSON 15

Using Context Clues (pages 61–64)

Objective: Children can use context clues to figure out unknown words.

Teaching TIPS

- Children improve comprehension by recognizing how to use context clues to figure out unfamiliar words.
- Children recognize that using context clues is an important reading strategy.

Skills Reviewed and Maintained

Comprehension
Using Details — See Teach
Drawing Conclusions — See Reading Passage 2

Phonics
Digraph *th* — See Practicing Vocabulary, Phonics Mini-Lesson

Writing
How-to Sentences — See Making the Reading and Writing Connection

Teach

Ask children if they ever hear or see words they don't understand. Encourage them to share their experiences. Then write these sentences on the board and read them aloud:

Most dogs <u>shed</u> hair. Their hair falls out.

- Point out that you can sometimes figure out the meaning of a word by looking for clues. Guide children to look for clues to help them figure out the meaning of the word *shed*.
- Tell children that sometimes they can understand a word they don't know by looking for details in pictures or word clues in the same sentence or another sentence. Then direct them to the activity on page 61.
- Review the first activity with children. Discuss how they were able to decide which word to choose to complete the sentence. Then have them complete the exercise on their own.
- Check for understanding by reviewing and discussing children's responses.

On Your Own Practice

Introducing Vocabulary

Before children read the passages, introduce the vocabulary words *(lose, teeth, mouth, bigger)* and help them look up their meanings in the Glossary.

Practicing Comprehension Skills

Reading Passage 1

- Review the illustration with children. Remind them that they can look for clues to the words they don't know in the pictures and sentences.
- Discuss the picture and word clues they used to decide which word belonged in each sentence.

Reading Passage 2

- Have children read the title and discuss the illustrations. Invite them to predict what "What Makes Baby Teeth Fall Out?" will be about.
- As children complete the activities, remind them to look for clues in the pictures and sentences. Encourage discussion of how they made their choices.
- Have children use the sentences and their own personal experiences to conclude that baby teeth fall out because you need bigger teeth as you grow.

Practicing Vocabulary

Ask children to identify the vocabulary words that end with the *th* sound. *(teeth, mouth)* After children complete the vocabulary exercise independently, review the answers as a group.

Apply

Making the Reading and Writing Connection

Call on volunteers to pretend they are dentists. Have them use their posters to tell their classmates about how to take

STRATEGY: Using Context Clues • **Lesson 15** T59

care of their teeth. Remind children to listen for clue words to understand the meanings of unfamiliar words.

You may want to refer to *The Write Direction* Grade 1 for additional opportunities in writing how-to sentences.

MEETING INDIVIDUAL NEEDS

Phonics: Digraph *th*
Write the vocabulary words *teeth* and *mouth* on the chalkboard.

- Say each word, emphasizing the /th/ sound as you underline those letters. Have children repeat the words. Repeat with the word *thumb*.

- Have children give the thumbs-up sign if they hear you say a word that begins with the /th/ sound as in *thumb*: think, sheep, time, thorn, thick, chin, toad, wheat, thirsty, chair, thirty, this, throat.

- Have children point to their mouth if they hear you say a word that ends with /th/ as in *mouth*: teeth, earth, fish, night, both, path, tent, peach, fifth, north, brush.

You may want to refer to pages 275–276 in *MCP Phonics*, Level A for additional practice with digraph *th*.

You may want to use the following *MCP Ready Readers*, Stage 0/1, Book 49, and Stage 2, Book 34, for more practice with digraph *th*.

ESL Strategy
Have children acquiring English highlight unfamiliar words in a paragraph or story. Then have partners work together to find context clues that help them figure out the meaning of the unfamiliar words.

Multiple Intelligences: Verbal-Linguistic, Interpersonal
Have children work in pairs. Tell each pair to think of a person, place, or thing, and make up a riddle to describe it; for example, *We write on it. It is white and has lines. What is it?* (paper) Invite children to share their riddles with the class.

Home-School Connection
Suggest to children that they play a "find the place" game with a family member. To play the game, they take turns giving clues to direct each other to a place in the home.

LESSON 16 Classifying (pages 65–68)

Objective: Children can identify how things are alike in order to classify them.

Teaching TIPS
- Classifying helps children recognize relationships in what they read.
- Classifying requires children to draw upon and apply information they already know.

Skills Reviewed and Maintained
Comprehension
Drawing Conclusions   See Teach
Using Details   See Reading Passage 1

Phonics
Final Blends   See Practicing Vocabulary, Phonics Mini-Lesson

Writing
Sentences   See Making the Reading and Writing Connection

Teach
Display pictures of food items that can be sorted into groups, such as fruits (apples, oranges, bananas), juices (orange, tomato, grape), and two or more kinds of cereal.

- Call on volunteers to put the pictures into groups. Use a prompt, such as "Which foods go together?" to get them started. Encourage children to explain their reasoning.

- Ask children which foods they would find together in a grocery store. Help them conclude that putting similar things together makes them easier to find.

- Discuss with children how things that are alike can go together and encourage them to offer examples of their own. Explain that as they read, they should also look for things that go together. Then work with them to complete the activities on page 65.

Lesson 16 • STRATEGY: Classifying

- After children complete the exercises, check for understanding by having them discuss the reasons for the choices they made.

 **Practice**

Introducing Vocabulary
Before children read the passages, introduce the vocabulary words *(pond, swim, seashore, found)* and discuss their meanings. Ask children to name words that come to mind when they hear each vocabulary word, for example, *pond: water, lake.*

Practicing Comprehension Skills

Reading Passage 1
- Discuss the details children already know about animals that live on land and animals that live in water. Remind them to look for ways things are alike as they read the story.
- After reading, review the chart. Have children identify the two ways they are going to group the animals. (land animals; water animals)

Reading Passage 2
- Direct children to read the story title on page 67. Ask them to look at the picture and predict what "Going to the Seashore" will be about.
- As children read the story, remind them to think about ways to group the things that are alike.
- After reading, review the chart and have children identify each of the three groups. When children finish, discuss their choices and how they made them.

Practicing Vocabulary
- Direct children to the words *pond* and *found.* Say each word, emphasizing the final *nd* blend. Have children identify the letters that make these sounds.
- After children complete the vocabulary exercise, review their answers together.

Apply

Making the Reading and Writing Connection
Ask volunteers to share their pictures and read their sentences. Suggest the name of another animal and ask children to tell why it would or would not belong in the picture.

You may want to refer to *The Write Direction* Grade 1 for additional opportunities in writing sentences.

MEETING INDIVIDUAL NEEDS

Phonics: Final Blends
Write *pond* at the top of two columns on the board.
- Circle the final blends and say each word slowly. Ask children to repeat the words and have them identify the letters that make the final sound.
- Then say *found* and *fish.* Ask children to tell which word has the same ending sound that they hear in *pond.* Write *found* under *pond.* Then help children write the words that have the final blend *nd* under the word *pond* after you say each one: *land, dash, and, wind, bed, send.*

You may want to refer to pages 253–55 in *MCP Phonics,* Level A for additional practice with final blends.

You may want to use the following *MCP Ready Readers,* Stage 2, Book 29 and Stage 3, Book 38 for more practice with final blends.

ESL Strategy
Display three objects, two of which can be grouped together. For example, a crayon, marker, and eraser. Have children identify and say the names of the two objects that belong together, and explain their choices.

Multiple Intelligences: Logical-Mathematical
Have children brainstorm things that land and water animals can do. Then help them use the Graphic Organizer on page T79 of this Guide to show ways that land and water animals are alike, different, and the same.

Home-School Connection
Suggest that children and a family member identify things around the house that can be grouped together, such as lamps, chairs, and toys.

STRATEGY: Classifying • Lesson 16 T61

Lesson 17: Comparing and Contrasting (pages 69–72)

Objective: Children can make comparisons and contrasts.

Teaching TIPS

- Children recognize that comparing and contrasting can help them use the known to figure out the unknown.
- Children appreciate that comparing and contrasting makes reading more interesting.

Skills Reviewed and Maintained

Comprehension
Drawing Conclusions — See Reading Passage 1
Making Predictions — See Reading Passage 2

Phonics
Endings: *ing* — See Practicing Vocabulary, Phonics Mini-Lesson

Writing
Sentences that Compare — See Making the Reading and Writing Connection

Teach

Show children a picture of a cat and a dog. Talk about each animal.

- Display the Graphic Organizer on page T79 of this Guide. Ask children to tell you some ways that dogs and cats are alike and different. Write their responses in the correct sections of the Venn Diagram.

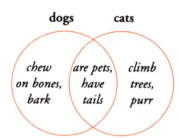

- Tell children that authors often use words and pictures to show how things are alike and different. Point out that *alike* means how things are the same, and *different* means how things are not the same.

- Direct children to the activity on page 69. Review and discuss the chart. Encourage children to verbalize how they know what is alike and what is different.

- Check for understanding by reviewing children's responses. You may wish to discuss with children how they know their colors. (Responses will probably be based on personal experience.)

 **Practice**

Introducing Vocabulary

Before children read the passages, introduce the vocabulary words *(talking, plants, green, living)* and discuss their meanings. Use the words in questions for children to answer. For example: *What plants grow in a garden? When do you enjoy talking?*

Practicing Comprehension Skills

Reading Passage 1

- Tell children that they are going to read a story about Sun and Moon. As they read, they should think about how the sun and moon are alike and different.

- After reading, have children complete the chart. When they finish, discuss how they decided which column to X.

- Help children conclude that Moon thought they were both best at what they do because they both do different things well.

Reading Passage 2

- Ask children to read the title and look at the illustration. Then have them predict what the story will be about.

- Remind children to look for things that are alike and different as they read. Have them complete the chart.

- Review children's responses. Have them identify words and sentences in the story that helped them complete the chart.

Practicing Vocabulary

Have children identify the two words that have the *ing* ending. *(talking, living)* Have children complete the exercise on their own. Then review the answers with the group.

Lesson 17 • STRATEGY: Comparing and Contrasting

Apply

Making the Reading and Writing Connection

Invite children to display their drawings as they read their sentences aloud. Have classmates listen for how things are alike and different and discuss their ideas.

You may want to refer to *The Write Direction* Grade 1 for additional opportunities in writing sentences that compare.

MEETING INDIVIDUAL NEEDS

Phonics: Endings: *ing*

Draw attention to the two vocabulary words with *ing* endings.

- Write the base words and ending on the chalkboard.

    talk + ing = talking   live + ing = living

    Guide children to see that silent *e* is dropped before the ending *ing* is added to *live*.

- Write these base words in a column on the chalkboard: *jump, smile, kick, walk, dance, sneeze, mix, grow, skate.*

- Call on a volunteer to choose a word and act it out. The child who guesses the word goes to the board and adds the *-ing* ending before choosing another word.

You may want to refer to pages 271–274 in *MCP Phonics*, Level A for additional practice with the ending *ing*.

You may want to use the following *MCP Ready Readers*, Stage 2, Book 1 and Stage 5, Book 2, for more practice with the ending *ing*.

ESL Strategy

Have partners work together to act out the movements of two familiar animals, such as a fish and a bird. First they dramatize ways in which the animals are alike. Then they show ways in which the animals are different.

Multiple Intelligences: Musical

Display a variety of musical instruments. Have children explore the instruments by looking at and playing them and listening to the sounds they make. Then work as a group to compare and contrast the instruments.

Home-School Connection

Suggest that children talk with family members during a meal about how various foods are alike and different.

Lesson 18: Author's Purpose (pages 73–76)

Objective: Children can identify the author's purpose for writing.

Teaching TIPS

- Recognizing the author's purpose will help children choose appropriate reading strategies.
- Recognizing the author's purpose will help children to better comprehend and appreciate what they read.

Skills Reviewed and Maintained

Comprehension

Making Predictions   See Reading Passages 1 and 2
Sequence of Events   See Reading Passage 1

Phonics

Short *o*   See Practicing Vocabulary, Phonics Mini-Lesson

Writing

Writing About a Game   See Making the Reading and Writing Connection

Teach

Display several books, some that tell a story and some that explain how to make things.

- Have children point to and say the author and title of each book.
- Flip through the books together, and discuss what each is about. Help children recognize that some of the books were written to tell stories and others were written to explain how to make things.

STRATEGY: Recognizing Author's Purpose • Lesson 18   T63

- Discuss with children that authors write books for different reasons. Invite them to suggest other reasons why someone might write a book. Then have them complete the activities on page 73.
- When children are finished, check for understanding by discussing their answers.

Practice

Introducing Vocabulary
Before children read the passages, introduce the vocabulary words *(stop, remember, sail, drop)* and discuss their meanings. Have children suggest antonyms for *stop* and *remember* and synonyms for *sail* and *drop*.

Practicing Comprehension Skills

Reading Passage 1
- Have children look at the title and illustration on page 74. Invite them to predict what these sentences will be about and why the author may have written them.
- After reading the sentences, review sequence of events by asking children to use the words *first, next, then,* and *last* to tell how to play *Hang Time*.
- Have children complete the exercises. Then review the answers together.

Reading Passage 2
- Have children use the title and cover illustration to predict what the story will be about.
- As children read the story, remind them to think about why the author wrote it. Ask: *Is the author telling you how to make or do something? Is he trying to make you laugh or smile?*
- After reading, have children complete the activities and review the answers. Then ask them how this story might have been different if the author had been trying to teach readers how to catch a ball. (He would have given step-by-step instructions and said things like *First, you . . .*)

Practicing Vocabulary
- Ask children to tell which vocabulary word has the short *o* sound. *(stop)*
- Direct children to complete the vocabulary exercise independently. Review the answers as a group.

Apply

Making the Reading and Writing Connection
Have children share their game drawings and sentences. Then ask them to explain their reason for writing.

You may want to refer to *The Write Direction* Grade 1 for additional opportunities in writing sentences.

MEETING INDIVIDUAL NEEDS

Phonics: Short o
Write the vocabulary word *stop* on the chalkboard.
- Say the word, emphasizing the short *o* sound. Have children say the word after you.
- Have volunteers underline the letter that stands for the short *o* sound.
- Give partners a soft ball. Have them toss the ball and stop when they hear a word with the short *o* sound. Say these words slowly, one at a time: *mop, hug, pet, got, shop, pin, pan, jog, top, hat, fox, sun, pot, dog, six, rock, box, let, hop, bib, rug, net.*

You may want to refer to pages 123–130 in *MCP Phonics*, Level A for additional practice with short *o*.

You may want to use the following *MCP Ready Readers*, Stage 2, Books 3, 9–12, 15, for more practice with short *o*.

ESL Strategy
Display books written in children's primary language. Then have pairs of children select and review a book. Invite them to tell the class the book's title and the author's name and describe his or her purpose for writing the book.

Multiple Intelligences: Visual-Spatial
Provide drawing paper and art materials for children to draw a cover for a book about dogs. Have them include a title and use their own name as the author. As children share their work, encourage them to tell their purpose for writing the book. *(to make readers laugh, to explain something, to make people think a certain way)*

Home-School Connection
Children can work with a family member to write three notes to post on the refrigerator or a family bulletin board. Each note should have a different purpose.

T64   Lesson 18 • STRATEGY: Recognizing Author's Purpose

Story Elements: Plot (pages 77–80)

Objective: Children can identify a story's plot.

Teaching TIPS

- Learning plot structure helps children predict what's happening next in a story.
- Learning plot structure helps children understand how a story is organized, which leads to better comprehension.

Skills Reviewed and Maintained

Comprehension
Sequence — See Reading Passage 1
Realism and Fantasy — See Reading Passage 2

Phonics
Contractions with *are* — See Practicing Vocabulary, Phonics Mini-Lesson

Writing
Story — See Making the Reading and Writing Connection

Teach

Read aloud a favorite story to children.

- Tell children that a story always has a beginning, a middle, and an end.
- Display the Graphic Organizer on page T74 of this Guide. Help children identify the beginning, middle, and end of the story you just read aloud. Write their responses on the chart.

Beginning:	The bears go for a walk because their soup is too hot.
Middle:	Goldilocks comes in. She eats the soup, breaks a chair, and takes a nap.
End:	The bears come home to find Goldilocks in their house. She jumps out the window and runs away.

- Invite children to identify the beginning, middle, and end of other stories they have heard or read.
- After children complete the exercise on page 77, check for understanding by having them discuss the reasons for their choices.

On Your Own Practice

Introducing Vocabulary

Before children read the passages, introduce the vocabulary words *(we're, prize, you're, hungry)* and discuss their meanings. Have children use the words in oral sentences.

Practicing Comprehension Skills

Reading Passage 1

- Ask children to look at the title and illustration on page 78 and predict what the plot will be about.
- Discuss children's answers to the exercises. Then direct them to draw pictures of the story's beginning, middle, and end on separate sheets of paper. Give children practice sequencing by having them arrange the drawings to show the order in which things happened.

Reading Passage 2

- Direct children to use the title and picture to predict what "Space Dog" will be about. Prompt them to tell what might happen in the beginning, middle, and end of this story.
- Review realism and fantasy by asking children to identify this as a real or a make-believe story. Encourage them to explain their choice.
- Guide children as they complete the activities on pages 79 and 80. Then review the answers with the group.

Practicing Vocabulary

Have children identify the two contractions with *are*. *(we're, you're)* After children complete the vocabulary exercises, go over their responses orally.

Apply

Making the Reading and Writing Connection

Have children share their stories about trips. After each

STRATEGY: Literary Elements: Plot • Lesson 19   T65

story is read, have groups of three retell the beginning, middle, and end, one story part per child.

You may want to refer to *The Write Direction* Grade 1 for additional opportunities in writing sentences.

MEETING INDIVIDUAL NEEDS

Phonics: Contractions with *are*
Write these words on the chalkboard: *we're = we are.*

- Explain that *we're* is written with a mark called an apostrophe. Explain that it takes the place of the letter *a* that was left out when *we* and *are* were put together.
- Tell children that words combined in this way are called contractions.
- Write each of these contractions on separate sheets of construction paper and tape them to the floor to make a path: *we're, they're, you're.*
- Have children walk along the path and name the two words each contraction stands for.

You may want to refer to pages 295–296 in *MCP Phonics,* Level A for additional practice with contractions with *are.*

You may want to use the following *MCP Ready Readers,* Stage 1, Book 50, for more practice with contractions with *are.*

ESL Strategy
Provide practice with the clue words *first, next, then,* and *finally.* Display the words, say them aloud, and model their meanings as you act out a common sequence of events, such as tying your shoes or opening a can. Then reread the story on page 79 and help children determine what happens *first, next, then,* and *finally.*

Multiple Intelligences: Bodily-Kinesthetic, Verbal-Linguistic
Have children draw stick figures to represent the characters in "Going to a Pet Show." Then glue the figures to craft sticks to use as puppets. Invite children to present the story as a puppet play. Children can hold up signs between the three acts labeled *beginning, middle,* and *end.*

Home-School Connection
Have children read a favorite story with a family member. Then retell what happens at the beginning, middle, and end of the story.

LESSON 20 Story Elements: Character (pages 81–84)

Objective: Children can identify a character's actions and feelings.

Teaching TIPS
- Children recognize that identifying a character's actions and feelings helps them understand what they read.
- Children appreciate that understanding a character's actions and feelings makes reading more interesting.

Skills Reviewed and Maintained

Comprehension
Drawing Conclusions   See Teach
Using Details   See Reading Passage 2

Phonics
Consonant Digraph *kn*   See Practicing Vocabulary, Phonics Mini-Lesson

Writing
Character Sketch   See Making the Reading and Writing Connection

Teach
Tell children that characters are the people or animals in stories. Explain that authors tell about what characters do and how they feel.

- Read the beginning of a familiar story to children such as:

    Little Red Riding Hood packed some brownies neatly in her bag. She was off to her Grandma's for a visit. She followed the trail to Grandma's house and gently knocked on the door.

Lesson 20 • STRATEGY: Literary Elements: Character

- Talk with children about the character in this story. Ask questions such as "Who is the character? What is she doing?" Then encourage them to use story details to draw conclusions about how the character feels.
- Direct children to the story on page 81. Remind them to think about who the character is and what the character is doing and feeling as they read. Then have children discuss each of these elements before completing the questions.
- After completing the activity, check children's understanding by having them identify elements in the story that helped them answer the questions.

 **Practice**

Introducing Vocabulary
Before children read the passages, introduce the vocabulary words *(anything, knight, brave, knew)*. Help children use the Glossary to find the meaning of each word.

Practicing Comprehension Skills

Reading Passage 1
- You may wish to read the poem aloud as children follow along. Encourage them to think about who the most important character is and what the character is doing and feeling.
- After reading, work with children to answer the questions. Encourage them to identify words and phrases in the poem that help them decide on an answer.

Reading Passage 2
- Invite children to predict what the poem will be about after reading the title and reviewing the illustration.
- Before reading, remind children to pay attention to story details that tell who the most important character is, what the character does, and how the character feels.
- After children complete the activity, discuss their responses. Encourage them to explain how they made their choices.

Practicing Vocabulary
Have children identify the two words that have the *kn* digraph. *(knight, knew)* Have children complete the exercise on their own. Review the answers with the group.

Apply

Making the Reading and Writing Connection
Call on volunteers to share their drawings and sentences with the class. Invite children to talk about who the character is, what the character is doing, and how the character is feeling.

You may want to refer to *The Write Direction* Grade 1 for additional opportunities in writing a character sketch.

MEETING INDIVIDUAL NEEDS

Phonics: Consonant Digraph *kn*
Write the words *knight* and *knew* on the chalkboard.

- Read the words and underline the *kn* digraph. Have children repeat the words. Guide children to understand that *kn* makes the same sound as *n* and that the *k* in *kn* is silent.
- Have children knock on their desks when they hear a word that begins with the /n/ sound: *know, chain, knee, wheel, sheep, knit, knife, chair, knot, knob, thumb, knuckles, knight, knew, knock.*
- As children knock, write each word on the chalkboard and underline the letters *kn.*

You may want to refer to pages 283–284 in *MCP Phonics*, Level A for additional practice with consonant digraph *kn.*

ESL Strategy
Children can draw pictures of "Pete and the King" that show what they do and how they feel. Display the pictures and help children brainstorm words to describe the characters.

Multiple Intelligences: Verbal-Linguistic
Have small groups of children talk about characters in fairy tales and folk tales, such as "Cinderella," "The Three Little Pigs," and "Goldilocks." Have each group write three sentences about one character they discuss. One sentence should tell who the character is, another should tell what the character is doing, and a third should tell how the character feels. Children can exchange sentences and identify which sentence tells what.

Home-School Connection
Have children read a story with a family member and then talk about one of the characters together. Suggest that they discuss how the character acts, thinks, and feels.

STRATEGY: Literary Elements: Character • Lesson 20 **T67**

Setting (pages 85-88)

Objective: Children can identify the setting of a story.

Teaching TIPS

- Children recognize that setting is an important story element.
- Children gain a better understanding of a story by being able to identify its setting.

Skills Reviewed and Maintained

Comprehension
Cause and Effect   See Reading Passage 1
Comparing and
  Contrasting   See Reading Passage 2

Phonics
Contractions with *will*   See Practicing Vocabulary, Phonics Mini-Lesson

Writing
Story   See Making the Reading and Writing Connection

Teach

Read the following sentences aloud: Jessica and Jason are at a place where they like to play. The snow is piled high on the swings. The slide is covered with ice. The afternoon sky is gray, and it looks like more snow will fall soon.

- Write the words *Where* and *When* on the chalkboard. Ask children to think about where and when the story you read takes place. Encourage them to share their ideas. Record their responses under the correct headings on the board.

- Point out to children that *where* and *when* a story happens is called the story's setting. Explain that a story can happen anyplace and anytime. Then direct them to the activity on page 85.

- Review and discuss the picture at the top of the page. Then have children complete the activity. When they finish, discuss their responses.

- Check for understanding by encouraging children to point out elements in the picture that helped them decide on their answers.

Practice

Introducing Vocabulary

Before children read the stories, introduce the vocabulary words (*I'll, windy, we'll, dinner*) and discuss their meanings. Have children categorize the words under the headings *Contractions, Meals, Weather*.

Practicing Comprehension Skills

Reading Passage 1

- Have children read "A Fish Story" on page 86. Remind them to think about when and where the story takes place as they read.

- After reading, review cause-and-effect relationships by asking children to complete this sentence: *Molly and her dad caught many fish because* _____ (the river was full of fish.)

- Have children complete the activity. Encourage them to identify elements in the story and picture that helped them with their answers.

Reading Passage 2

- Tell children to use the title and picture on page 87 to predict what the story will be about.

- Then have children read the story and discuss when and where it takes place.

- Have children complete the exercises on their own. Then review and discuss their responses. Resolve any differences by talking about elements in the story and picture that lead to the correct answers.

- Provide children an opportunity to compare and contrast settings by asking: How would this story be different if it took place on a hot summer day?

Practicing Vocabulary

Have children identify the two words that are contractions with *will*. (*I'll, we'll*) Children can complete the exercise on their own. Then review the answers with the group.

Lesson 21 • STRATEGY: Story Elements: Setting

Apply

Making the Reading and Writing Connection

Have children share their drawings and stories while classmates identify the settings. Create a class list showing the different settings children used.

You may want to refer to *The Write Direction* Grade 1 for additional opportunities in writing a story.

MEETING INDIVIDUAL NEEDS

Phonics: Contractions with *will*

Write *we'll* = *we will* on the chalkboard.

- Point out that *we'll* is written with a symbol called an apostrophe. Explain that the apostrophe takes the place of the letters *wi* that were left out when *we* and *will* are put together.

- Write the following words on cards and place them in a bag: *I'll, I will, we'll, we will, she'll, she will, he'll, he will, you'll, you will, they'll, they will.* Have each child draw a card, and then find the person with the matching card.

You may want to refer to pages 293–294 in *MCP Phonics*, Level A for additional practice with contractions with *will*.

You may want to use the following *MCP Ready Readers*, Stage 3, Books 1 and 8, for more practice with contractions with *will*.

ESL Strategy

Display magazine pictures that depict specific settings (a classroom, a playground, a city street). Have children describe each setting in their own words. Discuss stories that could happen in each setting.

Multiple Intelligences: Visual-Spatial

Have children use mural paper and colorful markers to show Molly and her dad in a different setting, such as a park, a movie theater, or a restaurant. Discuss how Molly and Dad's activities will be affected by the new setting.

Home-School Connection

As children read a story or watch a television show with a family member, suggest that they talk about where and when the story takes place.

LESSON 22: Alphabetizing (pages 89–92)

Objective: Children can alphabetize words by their first letter.

Teaching TIPS

- Children recognize that alphabetizing (ABC order) can be used to make things easier to find.
- Children recognize that alphabetizing is one way to order words.

Skills Reviewed and Maintained

Comprehension
Classifying — Reading Passage 1
Drawing Conclusions — See Reading Passage 2

Phonics
Long *i* — See Practicing Vocabulary, Phonics Mini-Lesson

Writing
Labels — See Making the Reading and Writing Connection

Teach

Using first names only, make a nametag for each child. Help children pin or tape the tags to the front of their clothing.

- Have children arrange themselves into groups according to the first letter of their name tags.

- Then arrange children in ABC order by saying: *Which group has names that start with A? Stand in line first. Which group has names that start with B? Stand in line next.* Repeat with the rest of the alphabet.

- When everyone is in line, explain that the line is in ABC order. Clarify that ABC order refers to things in the same order as the letters of the alphabet.

STRATEGY: Alphabetizing • Lesson 22 • T69

- Discuss why things like library books and children's names on a class list are arranged in ABC order. Lead children to see that ABC order makes things easier to find.
- Guide children as they work through the activity on page 89. Encourage them to look at the alphabet to help them fill in the missing letters.
- Check for understanding by discussing children's answers.

Practice

Introducing Vocabulary
Before children read the stories, introduce the vocabulary words (*march, size, rainbow, line*) and discuss their meanings. Have children use each word in oral sentences.

Practicing Comprehension Skills

Reading Passage 1
- Have children look at the illustration, title, and direction line on page 90. Invite them to predict how the children in this story might use ABC order.
- After reading, guide children as they complete the exercises. Remind them to look at the alphabet on the previous page if they need help.
- Review classifying by having children group story words by their initial letter (size, said, she; my, Meg, make; and so on)

Reading Passage 2
- Direct children to read the title of the story on page 91 and then look at the picture. Ask them to predict what is meant by "An ABC Rainbow."
- After children read the story, direct them to complete the exercises. Encourage them to say the alphabet aloud if they can't remember which letter comes first. Review and discuss their answers together.
- Help children conclude that this story is called "An ABC Rainbow" because the names of the colors the children used in their pictures are in ABC order.

Practicing Vocabulary
Ask children to tell which vocabulary words have the long *i* sound. (*size, line*) After children complete the vocabulary exercise independently, review the answers as a group.

Apply

Making the Reading and Writing Connection
Ask volunteers to share their ABC label book. Have classmates suggest another color for their book and help them decide where they would insert the new page.

You may want to refer to *The Write Direction* Grade 1 for additional opportunities in writing labels.

MEETING INDIVIDUAL NEEDS

Phonics: Long *i*
Write *size* and *line* on the chalkboard.
- Say each word aloud, emphasizing the long *i* sound. Have children repeat the words as you circle the letter *i* in each one.
- Tell children that long *i* is the same sound that they hear in *smile*.
- Then ask children to smile every time they hear a word with long *i*: *life, fine, bath, beach, prize, bike, boat, kite, wire, bug, wig, time, five*.

You may want to refer to pages 169–178 in *MCP Phonics*, Level A for additional practice with long *i*.

You may want to use the following *MCP Ready Readers*, Stage 2, Book 44; Stage 3, Books 4–6, 34; Stage 4, Books 12–14 for more practice with long *i*.

ESL Strategy
Provide a small group with an assortment of classroom objects. Have children take turns choosing three items, saying and writing their names, and then lining them up in ABC order.

Multiple Intelligences: Naturalist, Visual-Spatial
Have children collect and identify items from nature (or pictures of them), such as a leaf, a feather, and a pebble. Have them arrange and label the items in alphabetical order on a large piece of paper to create an "ABC Nature Mural."

Home-School Connection
Suggest that children work with a family member to write the names of neighborhood streets in ABC order.

Lesson 22 • STRATEGY: Alphabetizing

LESSON 23: Picture Map (pages 93–96)

Objective: Children can read a picture map.

Teaching TIPS

- Children recognize that reading picture maps provides important information about places.
- Children understand that using picture maps can make reading more enjoyable and interesting.

Skills Reviewed and Maintained

Comprehension
Using Details — See Reading Passage 1
Plot — See Reading Passage 2

Phonics
Short *e* — See Practicing Vocabulary, Phonics Mini-Lesson

Writing
Picture Map — See Making the Reading and Writing Connection

Teach

Tell children that they are going to help you draw a picture of the classroom.

- Draw a large rectangle on the board. Explain that this rectangle represents the classroom. Invite children to suggest things you should include in the picture, such as tables, desks, centers, trash can, and so on. Create a simple symbol for each item you include in the picture.

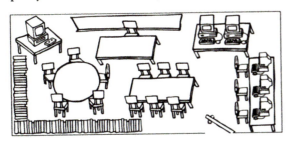

- Explain that this kind of picture is called a picture map. Model how to read the map by pointing to and naming various things on it.
- Direct children to look at the picture map on page 93. Have them identify what is shown on this map.

- Read the directions for each exercise and have children answer the questions. Check for understanding by having them explain their responses.

On Your Own Practice

Introducing Vocabulary

Before children read the passages, introduce the vocabulary words *(tent, tired, bench, slide)* and discuss their meanings. Have children categorize the words under these headings: *Places to Live, Feelings, Places to Sit.*

Practicing Comprehension Skills

Reading Passage 1

- Review the picture map and story title. Ask children what they think the picture map shows. Have them match details in the story with pictures on the map.
- After reading, review children's responses. Have them relate the choices they made to information in the story.

Reading Passage 2

- Direct children to read the poem on page 95. After children read the poem, have them complete the exercises on page 95 and 96. Encourage them to point to each answer on the map before they circle it.
- Review plot by writing the words *beginning, middle,* and *end* on the chalkboard. Invite children to tell what happened at each part of this poem.

Practicing Vocabulary

Ask children to point out the vocabulary words that have the short *e* sound. *(tent, bench)* After children complete the vocabulary exercise, review the answers as a group.

Apply

Making the Reading and Writing Connection

Call on volunteers to display their picture maps for the

STRATEGY: Reading a Picture Map • Lesson 23 T71

class. Have children tell what each map shows and discuss how they know.

You may want to refer to *The Write Direction* Grade 1 for additional opportunities in making picture maps.

MEETING INDIVIDUAL NEEDS

Phonics: Short e

- Draw and label a large tent on chart paper. Draw and label a large bench beside the tent.
- Read the labels aloud and underline in red the letter *e* in each word. Have children repeat the words.
- Tell children that the sound they hear in the middle of *tent, bench,* and *red* is the short *e* sound.
- Ask partners to search through classroom print sources to find other words that have the short *e* sound.
- Have children use red crayons to write the short *e* words they find on the tent or bench.

You may want to refer to pages 137–144 in *MCP Phonics*, Level A for additional practice with short *e*.

You may want to use the following *MCP Ready Readers*, Stage 2, Books 2, 5, 9, 13, 14, 16 for more practice with short *e*.

ESL Strategy

Have children acquiring English sit in a row facing you. Place a familiar object, such as a hammer in front of them. Place a nail next to the hammer. Say *The nail is to the right of the hammer.* Continue in this manner with other direction words such as *before, behind, under,* and so on. After modeling, have children do a similar exercise using familiar objects.

Multiple Intelligences: Visual-Spatial, Interpersonal

Provide children with large pieces of cardboard and craft materials, such as clay and wood. Direct small groups to design three-dimensional picture maps of the school playground and label each place on the playground map.

Home-School Connection

Children can work with a family member to draw and label a simple picture map of their neighborhood. Use the map to show how to get from one place to another.

LESSON 24 Picture and Bar Graphs (pages 97–100)

Objective: Children can interpret information on a picture and bar graph.

Teaching TIPS

- Children understand that picture and bar graphs are used to compare the number of things.
- Children recognize that picture and bar graphs can be used to find information quickly.

Skills Reviewed and Maintained

Comprehension
Using Details — See Reading Passage 1
Main Idea and Details — See Reading Passage 2

Phonics
Long o — See Practicing Vocabulary, Phonics Mini-Lesson

Writing
Bar Graphs — See Making the Reading and Writing Connection

Teach

Ask children to picture these animals and decide which is their favorite: *dog, cat, horse.* Have children vote for their favorite, and tally their responses on the chalkboard.

- Draw a bar graph grid, title, and labels on the chalkboard. Read each piece of information aloud.

Favorite Animal

Dog	🐶	🐶	🐶	🐶	🐶	🐶						
Cat	🐱	🐱	🐱	🐱								
Horse	🐴	🐴										
	1	2	3	4	5	6	7	8	9	10	11	12

Number of Children

Lesson 24 • STRATEGY: Using Picture and Bar Graphs

- Draw a bar or animal pictures to represent the number of children who voted for each animal. Ask children to help you decide where to stop drawing the bar.
- Explain that you have drawn a bar or picture graph. Explain that a bar graph is a picture that makes it easy to count and compare things.
- Ask children to look at the bar graph and answer questions such as *"Do more children like horses or dogs best?"*
- Direct children's attention to page 97 and guide them as they use the bar graphs to answer the questions.
- Check for understanding by discussing their responses.

Practice

Introducing Vocabulary
Before children read the passages, introduce the vocabulary words (*go, parade, show, families*) and discuss their meanings. Use these vocabulary words in questions and have children use the words in their answers.

Practicing Comprehension Skills

Reading Passage 1
- Have children look at the title, illustration, and bar graph to predict what this story will be about.
- After reading, tell children to look at the bar graph again. Help them identify the title, scale, and labels. Have them use details in the story and bar graph to answer the questions. Review the answers as a group.

Reading Passage 2
- After reading "How Many Songs?" review main idea and details by having them tell what the story is about.
- Direct children's attention to the bar graph, and ask them to identify the title and labels. Encourage discussion of the information shown in the graph.
- Have children complete the activities on pages 99 and 100. Have children explain their responses.

Practicing Vocabulary
Ask children to tell which vocabulary words have the long *o* sound. (*go, show*) Review the answers as a group after children complete the exercise independently.

Apply

Making the Reading and Writing Connection
Have children share their bar graphs. Then have them use their graphs to answer questions such as *"What instrument do most people want to play? How many children want to play the tuba?"*

You may want to refer to *The Write Direction* Grade 1 for additional opportunities in making bar graphs.

MEETING INDIVIDUAL NEEDS

Phonics: Long o
Write *go* and *show* on the board. Emphasize the long *o* sound as you say each word.

- Explain that these words have the same long *o* sound that children hear in *cone*.
- Brainstorm other words that have the long *o* sound and ask children to write these words on colorful paper circles that look like scoops of ice cream.
- Tape the scoops together to make a giant long *o* ice cream cone on the board. Read the words as a group.

You may want to refer to pages 199–210 in *MCP Phonics*, Level A for additional practice with long *o*.

You may use the following *MCP Ready Readers*, Stage 2, Book 45; Stage 3, Books 7–9, 18, 19, 31, 35, for more practice with long *o*.

ESL Strategy
Help children understand that a bar on a bar graph represents a number of items by drawing simple pictures of the items inside the bar. Children can count the items and trace their finger down to the number on the graph scale.

Multiple Intelligences: Visual-Spatial, Logical-Mathematical
Help children interpret information on a bar graph by having them line up counters to show how many items are represented by each bar. Then have partners ask each other questions about the information in the bar graph.

Home-School Connection
Children can work with a family member to make a bar graph to show and compare a number of items, such as knives, forks, and spoons; or different colors of socks.

STRATEGY: Using Picture and Bar Graphs • Lesson 24   173

GRAPHIC ORGANIZER

LESSON _____

Name _____

Story Sequence Chart

Read the story. Tell what happened in the beginning, the middle, and the end. Use words or pictures to retell the story.

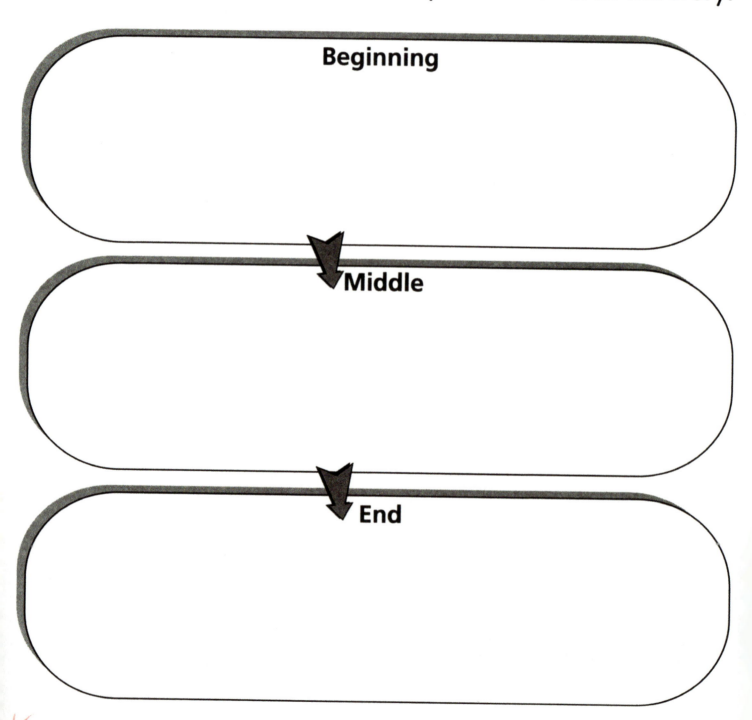

Comprehension Plus • Level A

GRAPHIC ORGANIZER

LESSON _____

Name _____

Summarizing Chart

Write one or two important ideas from the story. Then write a few sentences that include these ideas.

Important Idea

Important Idea

Summary

Comprehension Plus • Level A   75

GRAPHIC ORGANIZER Name _____ LESSON _____

Prediction Chart

What I predict will happen
_____
_____
_____
_____
_____
_____

What did happen
_____
_____
_____
_____
_____
_____

176 Comprehension Plus • Level A

GRAPHIC ORGANIZER

LESSON _____

Name _____

Main Idea and Details Chart

Read the story. Write in the first box what the story is about.
Then in the other boxes write words that tell about the main idea.

Main Idea

Detail

Detail

Comprehension Plus • Level A

GRAPHIC ORGANIZER   **LESSON** _____

Name _____

Cause and Effect Chart

1. What happened: _____

Why it happened: _____

~~~~~~~~~~~~~~~~~~~~~~~~~~~~~~~~~~~~~~

2. What happened: _____

Why it happened: _____

Comprehension Plus • Level A

GRAPHIC ORGANIZER   LESSON _____

Name _____

Venn Diagram

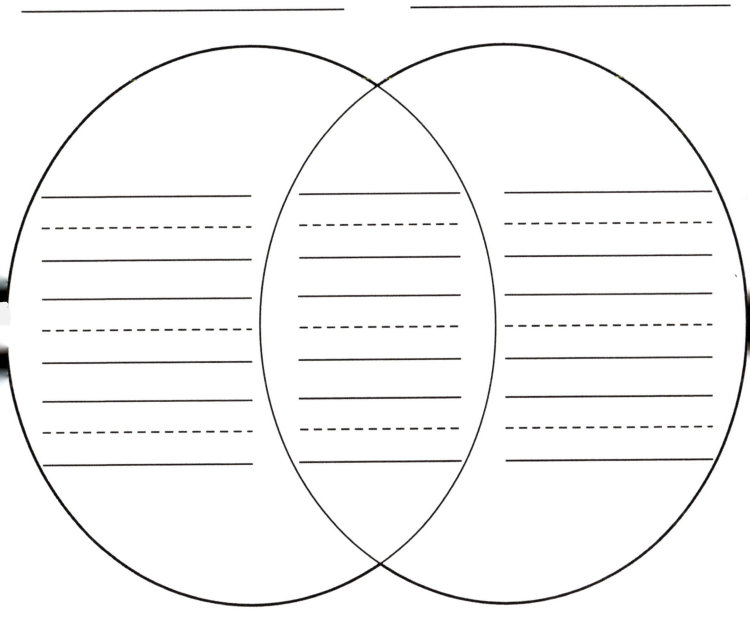

GRAPHIC ORGANIZER

LESSON _____

Name _____

Sequence of Events

Read the story. Think about the order of the things that happen. Use the lines to tell what happens first, next, and last.

First

Next

Last

T80   Comprehension Plus • Level A

Comprehension Plus
LEVEL A

Dr. Diane Lapp
Dr. James Flood

Modern Curriculum Press

All photographs ©Pearson Learning unless otherwise noted.

Photographs:

9: Upper, m.l. Peter Weinmann. 9: m.b. Johnny Johnson/Animals Animals. 9: m.r. Ron Sanford/Stone. 9: b.r., 71 t. Rich Iwasaki/Stone. 9: b.l. „Tom McHugh/Photo Researchers, Inc. 9: t.l. John Kieffer/Peter Arnold. 9: m.t. B. Lundberg/Bios/Peter Arnold, Inc. 9: t.r. R. Berenholtz/The Stock Market. 9: m.m, 11 upper „Jeff Lepore/Photo Researchers, Inc. 10: m. Stefan Meyers/Animals Animals. 10: t. Kathy Bushue/Stone. 10: b. Joel Bennett/Peter Arnold, Inc. 11: t.r. Donald Specker/Animals Animals. 11: t.l. Gary Vestal/Stone. 18: Chris Sorensen/The Stock Market. 19: E.R. Degginger/Bruce Coleman Inc. 21: t. Barbara Stitzer/PhotoEdit. 29: t.l., b.r. The Stock Market. 29: t.r. Ray Massey/Stone. 29: b.l. Peter Beck/The Stock Market. 29: m.t. Kathi Lamm/Stone. 29: m.b. Bill Miles/The Stock Market. 30: b. Michael Newman/PhotoEdit. 30: m. Jeff Greenberg/Peter Arnold, Inc. 30: m.b. Tom McCarthy/PhotoEdit. 50: Superstock, Inc. 51-52: Rocky Jordan/Animals Animals. 62: Helga Lade/Peter Arnold, Inc. 63: Tony Freeman/PhotoEdit. 63: m.l. Bob Thomas/Stone. 63: m.r David Young-Wolff/PhotoEdit. 63: l. Penny Gentieu/Stone. 65: r. „Steinhart Aquarium/Tom McHugh/the National Audubon Society Collection/Photo Researchers, Inc. 65: l. Stephen Frink/Stone. 65, 97: PhotoDisc, Inc. 66: t. Carl R. Sams II/Peter Arnold, Inc. 66: b. „E.R. Degginger/The National Audobon Society Collection/Photo Researchers, Inc. 69: l. Thomas Kitchin/Tom Stack & Assoc. 69: r. Walter H. Hodge/Peter Arnold, Inc. 71: b. Siede Preis/PhotoDisc, Inc.

Illustrations:

5-7, 93-95: Elizabeth Allen. 13-16, 49: Meredith Johnson. 25-27: Marisol Sarrazin. 33-35: Molly Delaney. 41-44: Anne Kennedy. 57-59: Pam Tanzey. 73-75: Anni Matsick. 45, 47: Betina Ogden. 37-40, 70: Erin Mauterer. 31-32, 77-80: Jeff LeVan. 81-83: Jhon Bendall-Brunello. 85-87: Laurie Struck Long.

Cover art: photo montage: Wendy Wax. background: Doug Bowles.

Design development: MKR Design, New York: Manuela Paul, Deirdre Newman, Marta K. Ruliffson.

Design: John Maddalone

Copyright © 2002 by Pearson Education, Inc., publishing as Modern Curriculum Press, an imprint of Pearson Learning Group, 299 Jefferson Road, Parsippany, NJ 07054. All rights reserved. No part of this book may be reproduced or transmitted in any form or by any means, electronic, or mechanical, including photocopying, recording, or by any information storage and retrieval system, without permission in writing from the publisher. For information regarding permission(s), write to Rights and Permissions Department. This edition is published simultaneously in Canada by Pearson Education Canada.

ISBN: 0-7652-2180-2

Printed in the United States of America

12 13 14 15   09 08 07 06

1-800-321-3106
www.pearsonlearning.com

Table of Contents

Comprehending Text

Lesson 1:	Following Directions	5
Lesson 2:	Using Details	9
Lesson 3:	Main Idea	13
Lesson 4:	Main Idea and Details	17
Lesson 5:	Summarizing	21
Lesson 6:	Drawing Conclusions	25
Lesson 7:	Drawing Conclusions	29
Lesson 8:	Sequence of Events	33
Lesson 9:	Sequence of Events	37
Lesson 10:	Predicting Outcomes	41
Lesson 11:	Predicting Outcomes	45
Lesson 12:	Cause and Effect	49
Lesson 13:	Cause and Effect	53
Lesson 14:	Real and Make-Believe	57
Lesson 15:	Using Context Clues	61
Lesson 16:	Classifying	65
Lesson 17:	Comparing and Contrasting	69
Lesson 18:	Author's Purpose	73

Story Structure

Lesson 19: Plot 77
Lesson 20: Character 81
Lesson 21: Setting 85

Word Study

Lesson 22: Alphabetizing 89

Document Reading

Lesson 23: Picture Maps 93
Lesson 24: Picture and Bar Graphs 97
Glossary 101

Lesson 1: Following Directions

Directions tell you what to do.
Following directions can help you do things.
You follow many directions every day.

Please pack the bag.

Get in the van, please.

You follow other kinds of directions at school.

Follow this direction.

● Draw a circle around the word that matches the picture.

ball

box

Try following another direction.

■ Draw a line under the word that matches the picture.

shell

pail

Tip **Directions help you know what to do. Here are some direction words: draw a line, draw a circle, write, fill in, look, read.**

STRATEGY: Following Directions 5

Practicing Comprehension Skills

Read the sentences.
Think about what the directions tell you to do.

Mix sand and water.

Put the wet sand in a pail.

Turn the pail over.

You just made a sand castle!

1. Draw a circle around the things you need to make a sand castle.

2. Draw a line under the picture that shows where to put the sand.

3. What do the directions say to do first? Draw a box around the sentence.

   Put wet sand in a pail.   Turn the pail over.

   Mix sand and water.

Lesson 1

Read the sentences.
Think about the directions.

Let's Go Fishing

First, get a fishing pole and a worm.
Put the worm on the hook.
Then drop the hook into the water.
Soon you will catch a fish!

4. You want to go fishing.
   Draw a circle around the thing you need.

5. What do you put on the hook?
   Draw a box around it.

6. Where do you drop the hook?
   Draw a line under it.

STRATEGY: Following Directions

7. Write the word that belongs in the sentence.

The children use a pole to go ___*fishing*___ .

dancing   fishing   skating

Practicing Vocabulary

Write a word from the box on each line.

sand   catch   water   worm

8. Put a ___*worm*___ on your hook.

9. You can dig in the ___*sand*___ .

10. You can ___*catch*___ a fish.

11. You can swim in the ___*water*___ .

Use another piece of paper.
Draw a picture of you at the beach.
Write a sentence about your picture.

LESSON 2 Using Details

Do you like to look at pictures? Sometimes pictures can tell a story.

This picture tells a story.

Read each question.
Circle the picture that tells the answer.

● Where is the bear?

■ What is the bear doing?

▲ What does the bear use to climb?

Tip Pictures can help you when you read. When you look at a picture, think about all the things you see. Try to remember them.

STRATEGY: Using Details 9

Practicing Comprehension Skills

Bear Cubs

Look at each picture.
Draw a circle around the sentence that goes with the picture.

1.    Bear cubs stay away from their mother.
   (Bear cubs stay near their mother.)

2.    (The cubs learn how to find fish.)
   The cubs learn how to fight.

3.   (The cubs like to play.)
   The cubs like to read.

Write the word that belongs in the sentence.

4. Bear cubs stay close to their ___mother___ .

   mother   food   friends

10   Lesson 2

Read the sentences. Look at the pictures.
Think about what they tell you.

# Time to Eat

Bears catch and eat fish.

Bears like fruit.

Bears like nuts.

Bears like honey, too!

Read each question.
Draw a circle around the picture that tells the answer.

5. What do bears catch and eat?

6. What do bears like to eat?

7. What else do bears like to eat?

8. Do bears eat honey?
   Draw a line under the answer.   yes   no

STRATEGY: Using Details   11

Write the word that belongs in the sentence.

9. Bears eat many kinds of ___food___ .

        trees   food   rocks

Practicing Vocabulary

Draw a line from the word to the clue it matches.

10. **nuts**   big animals that live in forests

11. **bears**   animals that live in the water

12. **cubs**   food that has a shell

13. **fish**   baby bears

Use another piece of paper. Draw a picture of an animal you like. Write a sentence that tells about the animal.

Lesson 2

Main Idea

What is the main idea?
The main idea is what a story is all about.
To find the main idea, think about what the whole story is about.

Draw a line under the sentence that tells what each picture is about.

● Matt has a new book.

Matt has a new pet.

■ Little Mouse lives in the country.

Little Mouse lives in the city.

▲ The dog has a ball.

The dog has a bone.

 Tip | **Sometimes one picture or one sentence tells the main idea. Sometimes the name of the story tells the main idea.**

STRATEGY: Identifying the Main Idea 13

Practicing Comprehension Skills

Read the story.
Look for a sentence that tells the main idea.

Jane has a new toy bird.
She likes to play with it.
Jane makes the bird go up and down.
She helps the bird fly.

Think about the story. Then read each sentence.
Does the sentence tell the main idea of the story?
Write **yes** or **no**.

1. She helps the bird fly. _____no_____

2. Jane has a new toy bird. _____yes_____

3. Jane makes the bird go up and down. _____no_____

4. Draw a line under the best name for the story.

   <u>Jane's New Toy</u>   Birds Can Fly   Jane Sees a Bug

Lesson 3

Read the poem. Think about the main idea.

A butterfly goes by.
It flies up in the sky.
I see it fly away.
Come back another day.

Fill in the circle next to the right answer.

5. What is the poem all about?

○ The sky   ○ A flower   ● A butterfly

6. Which sentence tells the main idea?
Write it on the lines.

It is flying in the sky.

A butterfly goes by.

It will come back again.

I see it fly away.

A butterfly goes by.

STRATEGY: Identifying the Main Idea   15

7. What is the best name for the poem?
Draw a line under it.

<u>The Butterfly</u>   Blue Sky   Pretty Flower

Practicing Vocabulary

Write a word from the box on each line.

| sky | another | bird | fly |

8. I see a plane in the ___<u>sky</u>___ .

9. The ___<u>bird</u>___ is in a tree.

10. Some bugs can ___<u>fly</u>___ .

11. I will read ___<u>another</u>___ book.

Use another piece of paper. Draw a picture of your favorite animal doing something. Write a name for your picture that tells the main idea.

16   Lesson 3

LESSON 4: Main Idea and Details

You can learn a lot from stories. The main idea is the most important idea you learn. It tells what the sentences or pictures are all about.

Read the story and look at the picture.

This is Sara's first airplane ride.
She sits with Woolly Bear.
They look out the window.
Sara thinks flying is fun!

● Circle the name that belongs in the sentence.

Sara sits with _____.

Mom   (Woolly Bear)

■ Draw a line under the word that tells what the story is all about.

playing   flying   looking

Tip: Try to remember all the things a story tells. To find the main idea, think about what the picture or story is all about.

STRATEGY: Main Idea and Details

Practicing Comprehension Skills

Read the sentences.
Think about what they tell you.

A pilot flies a plane.
Pilots go to school to learn how to fly.
They learn how to read maps.
They learn about weather.
Then pilots can fly planes to many places.

Draw a circle around the correct words.

1. To fly a plane, pilots go to _____.

   a park   (school)   the store

2. Draw a line under the sentence that tells what the sentences are all about.

   Pilots learn about air.

   <u>Pilots have to learn many things.</u>

   Pilots learn how to read books.

3. Draw a line under the best name for the sentences.

   Reading Maps   Big Planes   <u>A Pilot's Job</u>

Lesson 4

Read the sentences.
Think about what the sentences tell you.

Did you ever see a blimp?
Blimps look very different than planes.
The top part is like a big balloon.
This part is filled with a gas.
The gas makes the blimp float in the air.
The bottom part is like a small box.
This is where the people sit.
Would you like to fly in a blimp?

Fill in the circle next to each correct answer.

4. What do blimps look like?

   ● big balloons   ○ apples   ○ small boxes

5. Where do the people sit?

   ○ in the top   ○ on a balloon   ● in the bottom

6. The top part of a blimp is filled with

   ○ oranges.   ● gas.   ○ boxes.

7. Draw a line under the sentence that tells the main idea.

   <u>Learn about blimps.</u>   Blimps are balloons.

   Blimps are big.

STRATEGY: Main Idea and Details   19

8. Circle the best name for the sentences.

   Flying Things   Blimps Are Big   (All About Blimps)

Practicing Vocabulary

Write the word from the box that matches each clue.

balloon	blimp	pilot	plane

__blimp__ 9. big flying machine that floats in the air

__plane__ 10. flying machine with wings

__balloon__ 11. something filled with air

__pilot__ 12. person who flies a plane

Use another piece of paper. Draw a picture of something that can fly. It can be a bird, a plane, a balloon, or a blimp. Then write a sentence that tells about your picture.

Lesson 4

Lesson 5: Summarizing

When you tell about a story, you tell the important parts. You leave out the parts that are not important. You tell what the story is all about.

Read these sentences.
Think about what is important.

People wear all kinds of clothes.
When it is cold they wear hats and mittens.
When it is hot they wear shorts.
When it rains they wear boots.

People need different clothes for different kinds of weather.

- Draw a line under the sentence that tells the most important parts.

<u>People wear different clothes in hot and cold weather.</u>

People wear boots when there is snow outside.

Tip: When you tell what something is all about, you tell only the most important parts.

STRATEGY: Summarizing

Practicing Comprehension Skills

Read the sentences.
Think about the important parts.

Lots of Hats

There are many different kinds of hats.
Some hats have flaps to keep ears warm.
Some hats are wide to give shade from the sun.
A hard hat keeps a worker's head safe
Some hats show the jobs people do.

Draw a line under the best answer.

1. Are all hats the same?   Yes   Maybe   <u>No</u>

2. How do hats help people?

   <u>Hats keep ears warm.</u>   Hats keep hands safe.

   Hats keep toes warm.

3. What is the most important thing about "Lots of Hats"?

   Some people do not like to wear hats.

   Some hats look funny.

   <u>There are many different kinds of hats.</u>

Lesson 5

Read the sentences.
Think about what is important.

Working Shoes

Shoes can help people do their jobs.
Boots keep a firefighter's feet dry.
Sneakers help players run and jump.
Heavy boots keep a worker's feet safe.
Different workers use different kinds of shoes.

Fill in the circle next to the best answer.

4. What can shoes help people do?

● their jobs ○ homework ○ wash dishes

5. What is "Working Shoes" mostly about?

○ socks ● different shoes ○ sneakers

6. What is one kind of shoe "Working Shoes" tells about?

○ slippers ○ sandals ● boots

STRATEGY: Summarizing

7. Draw a line under the sentence that tells the most important thing about "Working Shoes."

<u>Different kinds of shoes help workers do their jobs.</u>

Some workers have too many pairs of shoes.

Some workers need boots.

Practicing Vocabulary

Draw a line from the word to the group it belongs with.

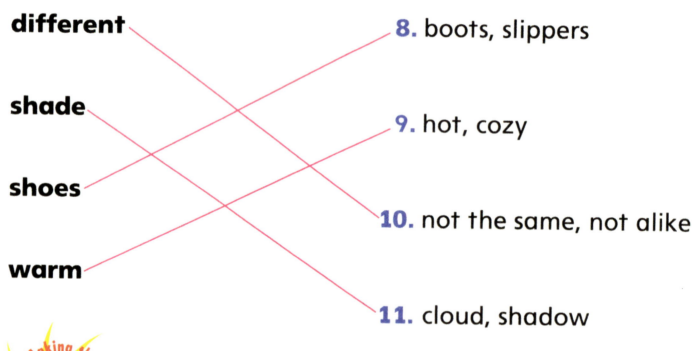

different — 10. not the same, not alike
shade — 11. cloud, shadow
shoes — 8. boots, slippers
warm — 9. hot, cozy

On another piece of paper, draw a picture of your favorite kind of shoes or clothes. Write a sentence that tells about your picture.

Lesson 5

Lesson 6: Drawing Conclusions

When you read, look for picture and word clues. Think about what you already know. Put it all together to help you understand what you read.

Look at this picture. What do you see? You know that kittens like to be petted. How do you think the kitten feels?

- Draw a line under the sentence that tells how the kitten feels.

   <u>The kitten is happy.</u>   The kitten is not happy.

- Look for clues in the picture. Draw a line under the sentence that tells about the picture.

Toby will play outside today.

<u>Toby will play inside today.</u>

Tip: When you read, look at the pictures and words. Think about all the clues you find. Put them together with what you already know.

STRATEGY: Drawing Conclusions 25

Practicing Comprehension Skills

Read the story and look at the picture.
Think about the clues.

Kim and Mom are going on a visit.
On the way Kim sees some flowers.
She stops to smell them.
She decides to pick some.
Soon Kim knocks at a door.
"Hello, Grandma," says Kim.
"These are for you!"

Draw a line under the correct answer.

1. Who is Kim going to visit?

   <u>her grandmother</u>   her mother   a friend

2. Why does Kim pick some flowers?

   She wants to give them to her mother.

   She wants to give them to a friend.

   <u>She wants to give them to her grandmother.</u>

Lesson 6

Read the story. Look at the picture.
Think about the clues.

Bill Tries to Sleep

Bill is a pig who cannot sleep.
"What is that smell?" he asks.
"Please quit singing," he says.
Bill shuts the window.
Then he falls asleep at last.

Fill in the circle next to the right answer.

3. What does Bill hear?

   ○ a skunk   ● a cat   ○ a pig

4. What does Bill smell?

   ○ a window   ○ a cat   ● a skunk

5. Why does Bill shut the window?
   Draw a line under the sentence that tells why.

   He wants to work.

   It is cold in the room.

   <u>He wants to sleep.</u>

STRATEGY: Drawing Conclusions

Read the question. Draw a line under two sentences that tell the answer.

6. Why do you think Bill falls asleep?

   <u>Bill does not hear the cat singing.</u>

   <u>Bill does not smell the skunk.</u>

   Bill does not shut the window.

Practicing Vocabulary

Write the word that belongs in each group.

7. taste, hear, _____smell_____

8. rest, nap, _____sleep_____

9. choose, keep, _____pick_____

10. stop, halt, _____quit_____

| sleep |
| smell |
| quit |
| pick |

On another piece of paper, write some clues that tell about a food you like. Tell how it looks, tastes, and smells. Have a friend guess your food.

Lesson 6

LESSON 7
Drawing Conclusions

How do you find the answer to a riddle?
First, you read each clue.
Then you put all the clues together.
You think about them again.
You find the answer.

● Read the riddles.
Draw a line under the answers.

I take care of animals.
I help them feel better when they are sick.
Who am I?

a teacher   <u>a vet</u>   a clown

I like to help children.
I teach them many things.
Who am I?

a dentist   a builder   <u>a teacher</u>

Tip Think about clues when you read. Think about things you already know. Put them together to help you understand what you read.

STRATEGY: Drawing Conclusions

Practicing Comprehension Skills

Read each riddle about someone's job. Draw a line from the riddle to the picture that answers it.

1. I carry a huge bag full of letters.
   I bring the letters to people.
   Who am I?

2. I work on an airplane.
   I take people places.
   Who am I?

3. I work with sick people.
   I help them feel better.
   Who am I?

4. I work in a shop.
   I cut people's hair.
   Who am I?

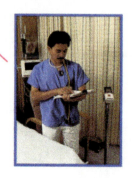

Lesson 7

Read the story.
Look for clues in the words and pictures.

The Missing Ring

"Use this rake," said Mr. Lee.
"I like to help you work," said Sue.
"Take off your ring while we work," said Mr. Lee.
"I will hang it up," said Sue.
Later, Sue could not find her ring.
"Where is it?" she cried.

Fill in the circle next to the correct answer.

5. What work are Sue and Mr. Lee doing?

    ○ making a nest   ● raking leaves   ○ sweeping

6. Where did Sue put her ring while she worked?

    ○ on the ground   ○ around her neck   ● on a tree

7. Who took Sue's ring?
   Draw a line under the picture.

STRATEGY: Drawing Conclusions

8. Where will Sue find her ring?
Draw a circle around the picture.

Practicing Vocabulary

Write the word from the box that matches each clue.

| use | ring | huge | letters |

___letters___ **9.** things that come in the mail

___huge___ **10.** very big

___use___ **11.** to do something with

___ring___ **12.** something you wear on your finger

On another sheet of paper, write a riddle. Give two or three clues about a job someone does. Ask a friend to answer your riddle.

32 Lesson 7

Sequence of Events

In a story, things happen in order. Something happens first. Something happens next. Something happens last. When you read, think about the order of the things that happen.

These pictures tell a story in order.

- These pictures show what Dee made in art class. These pictures are not in order. Write 1, 2, or 3 next to each picture to show what happened first, next, and last.

__2__  __3__  __1__

 Tip Think about the order of the things that happen in a story. What happens first? What happens next? What happens last?

STRATEGY: Sequence of Events

Practicing Comprehension Skills

Read the story.
Think about what happens first, next, and last.

Dee and Robo

One night, Dee had a dream about Robo.
First, Robo went to the kitchen.
Next, Robo made breakfast for Dee.
Last, Robo washed the dishes.

1. Write words from the box to put the pictures in order.

_____ last _____   _____ first _____   _____ next _____

34 Lesson 8

Read the story. Think about the order of what happens.

A Buzzy Day

Ben has a friend named Buzzy.
First, Buzzy eats with Ben.
Then, Buzzy rides the bus with Ben.
At school, Buzzy reads with Ben.
Last, Buzzy goes to sleep with Ben.

2. Draw a line from the sentences to the numbers to show when things happen.

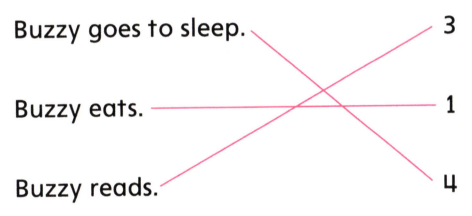

Buzzy goes to sleep. — 3

Buzzy eats. — 1

Buzzy reads. — 4

Buzzy rides the bus. — 2

3. What happens after Buzzy rides the bus? Draw a circle around the correct picture.

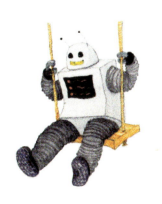

STRATEGY: Sequence of Events

4. What happens before Buzzy rides the bus?
   Draw a line under the correct sentence.

   <u>Buzzy eats.</u>   Buzzy goes to school.

Practicing Vocabulary

Write the word from the box that belongs in each group.

5. bedroom, den, _____kitchen_____

6. teacher, classroom, _____school_____

7. draws, writes, _____reads_____

8. night, sleep, _____dream_____

| dream |
| kitchen |
| reads |
| school |

Pretend a robot visited you. On another piece of paper, draw three pictures. Show what you and the robot do. Write 1, 2, and 3 to show what happens first, next, and last.

Lesson 8

Sequence of Events

When you read, think about the order of things. Something happens first. Then something else happens. Try to remember the order of the things that happen.

- These pictures tell a story.
  The sentences tell the same story.
  Write 1, 2, 3, and 4 next to each sentence to show the order.

__4__ The cake is gone.

__2__ Cow gets a cake.

__1__ Frog comes to visit.

__3__ They eat cake.

 Tip When you read, use clue words to help you. Words such as first, then, next, and last can help you remember the order.

STRATEGY: Identifying Sequence of Events

Practicing Comprehension Skills

Read the story.
Think about the order of the things that happen.

A Special Day

First, Jane made a cake.
Then, she went to find her dad.
"Come outside with me," Jane said.
"Now close your eyes," Jane said.
At last Jane shouted, "Happy birthday!
You can open your eyes!"

1. Show the order of things that happened in "A Special Day." Write 1, 2, 3, or 4 on the lines.

   _4_

   _2_

   _1_

   _3_

Read the story.
Think about the order of the things that happen.

Sam's Surprise
by Cheryl Chapman

First, Kate made a map for Sam.
Sam read the map.
It led to a table.
Next, Sam saw two plates.
There was cake on the plates.
Then, Kate said, "Happy birthday, Sam!"
"This is good cake!" Sam said at last.

2. Read the sentences.
   Write 1, 2, 3, or 4 on the lines to show the order of things that happened.

Sam saw cake. __3__   Sam read the map. __2__

They ate cake. __4__   Kate made Sam a map. __1__

STRATEGY: Identifying Sequence of Events

3. What did Kate do last? Fill in the circle.

　　○ She baked a cake.

　　● She said, "Happy Birthday, Sam!"

　　○ She made a map.

Practicing Vocabulary

Write a word from the box on each line.

4. Kate put the ___plates___ in the sink.

5. Sam loves to eat birthday ___cake___ .

6. "I want the ___first___ piece!" cried Pig.

7. Jane ___made___ a big mess!

| made |
| cake |
| first |
| plates |

On another sheet of paper, draw three pictures about a birthday party. Write a story about the pictures. Use words like first, then, and last to show when things happen.

Lesson 9

Predicting Outcomes

Do you ever wonder what will happen next in a story? Clues in the words and pictures may tell you.

● Molly is dressed to go outside.

What will Molly do next?
Draw a circle around the picture.

■ Molly likes to make things with snow.

What will Molly do next?
Draw a line under the picture.

| Tip | When you read, think about what will happen next. Look for word and picture clues. They will help you. |

STRATEGY: Predicting Outcomes

Practicing Comprehension Skills

Read the story. Then tell what happens next.
Look for clues in the sentences.

Ups and Downs
by Robin Pulver

Sam's sled went down, down, down the snowy hill.
"Oh, no!" Sam said.
"Now I have to pull my sled back up."
Sam wanted to go down again.

1. What will Sam do next?
   Draw a circle around the picture.

Soon, Sam's feet and hands got cold.
His nose was cold, too.
It was almost time for lunch.
Jill said, "Let's ride down again."

2. What will Sam do now?
   Draw a circle around the picture.

Lesson 10

Read the story below.
Think about what will happen next.

Frosty Friends

"Help! I'm stuck inside," said Fuzzy Tail.
"There's too much snow!"
"I have a shovel to help you," said Owl.
"Thank you, Owl," Fuzzy Tail said.
"All this work makes me hungry," said Owl.
"Now I will help you," said Fuzzy Tail.
"Yum!" said Owl.

Draw a circle around your answer.

3. How will Owl help Fuzzy Tail?

4. How will Fuzzy Tail help Owl?

STRATEGY: Predicting Outcomes 43

5. What will Fuzzy Tail and Owl do next?
Draw a line under the picture.

Practicing Vocabulary

Draw a line from the sentence to the word it is missing.

6. The boy needed ____ to get up.

again

7. It is fun to play in the ____ .

snow

8. A ____ goes down the hill.

help

sled

9. The boy went home ____ .

On another sheet of paper, start a story. Write your story about playing outside with a friend. Ask your friend to tell what will happen next.

Predicting Outcomes

You can tell what will happen next in a story.
Think about what you already know.
Picture clues and word clues can help you, too.

Look at the pictures.
Draw a line under the sentence that
tells what will happen next.

<u>They ride in a boat.</u>
They get in a car.

Dad will splash Sally.
<u>The fish will splash Sally.</u>

Tip To tell what will happen next in a story, ask, "What do I already know?" Putting all the clues together will help you.

STRATEGY: Predicting Outcomes 45

Practicing Comprehension Skills

Read the story.
Think about what will happen next.

 Whale Watch

Bob and Mom are on a big boat.
They want to see a whale.
"Look!" says the boat captain.
Bob and Mom see a spray of water.

Fill in the circle next to the answer.

1. What do you think the spray of water means?

    ○ A bird is flying by.   ○ It is raining.

    ● A whale is under the water.

2. What do you think will happen next?

    ○ They will go home.   ● They will see a whale.

    ○ They will see the moon.

3. How will Bob and Mom feel when they see the whale?

    ○ tired   ● happy   ○ sad

Read the story.
Look for clues to tell what will happen next.

Wet Like Whales

"The whales are so close!" said Bob.
"Wear these raincoats," the captain said.
"Why?" asked Bob's mother.
"You'll see!" laughed the captain.

Draw a line under the answer.

4. Why do you think the captain gives Bob and Mom raincoats?

She wants them to stay warm.

<u>She wants them to stay dry.</u>

She wants them to eat.

5. What do you think will happen when the whale leaps out of the water?

<u>Water will splash on Bob and Mom.</u>

Bob and Mom will jump in the water.

Bob and Mom will fly in the air.

STRATEGY: Predicting Outcomes

6. What will Bob say when he gets home?
   Draw a line under the sentence.

   <u>I saw some whales!</u>

   I saw some birds!

   I saw a tiger!

Practicing Vocabulary

Write the word from the box that belongs in each group.

	whale
7. leader, chief, __captain__	captain
8. when, where, __why__	why
9. fish, shark, __whale__	raincoats
10. hats, boots, __raincoats__	

On another sheet of paper, write an animal story. Read the first part to a friend. Let your friend tell how the story ends.

Lesson 11

Cause and Effect

When you read, think about what happens.
Think about why it happens.

Think about what happens in each picture.

The children play.   It begins to rain.   They go inside.

Sometimes when one thing happens, it makes something else happen. Now read these sentences.

The bug lands on Becky.
Becky waves her arm.

● **Draw a circle to show what happens next.**

Tip   When you read, think about how one thing can make another thing happen.

STRATEGY: Recognizing Cause-and-Effect Relationships

Practicing Comprehension Skills

Read the sentences.
Think about what happens and why.

Bees get food from flowers.
A bee takes the food back to the hive.
Then the bee dances for the other bees.
The dance tells the other bees where to find food.
Bees look for food in warm weather.
In cold weather, bees stay in the hive.
Then they eat the honey stored in the hive.

Read the first part of each sentence.
Draw a line under the words that tell
what happens next.

1. Bees need food, so

   they go to a store.   they get it from flowers.   they buzz.

2. When a bee finds food,

   it dances to tell the others.   it flies away.   it hides.

3. When it is cold,

   bees sleep.   bees fly away.   bees stay in the hive.

Read the sentences.
Think about what happens and why.

A Snack for a Spider

Spiders make webs.
They use the webs to catch bugs.
A spider's web is like a sticky net.
When a bug flies into the web, it gets stuck.
Then the spider eats the bug.

Read the first part of each sentence.
Then fill in the circle next to the words
that tell what happens next.

4. The spider makes a web, so

　○ it flies away.　● it catches bugs.　○ it falls asleep.

5. Because the web is sticky,

　○ it glows.　○ bugs see it.　● bugs get stuck.

6. A spider catches a bug, and then it

　● eats it.　○ hugs it.　○ sings to it.

7. When a bug flies into the web,

　○ it runs away.　○ it smells pretty.

　　　　● it gets stuck.

STRATEGY: Recognizing Cause-and-Effect Relationships

Draw a line under the correct sentence.

8. Why do spiders catch bugs?

Spiders play with bugs.

<u>Spiders eat bugs.</u>

Spiders spin bugs.

Practicing Vocabulary

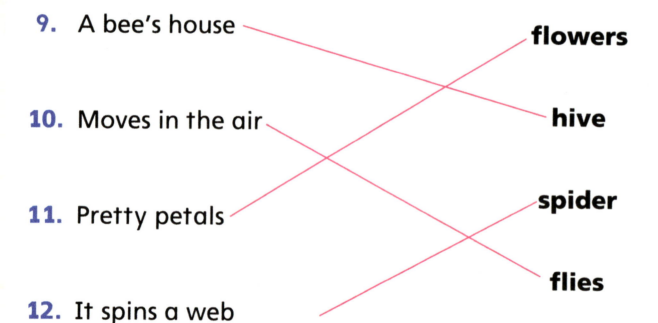

Draw a line from the clue to the word.

9. A bee's house — flowers

10. Moves in the air — hive

11. Pretty petals — spider

12. It spins a web — flies

(9 → hive, 10 → flies, 11 → flowers, 12 → spider)

Think about something a bug does. On another piece of paper, draw a picture of it. Write sentences that tell why the bug does it.

Lesson 12

LESSON 13 Cause and Effect

When you read, think about what happens. Then think about why things happened. Look for words such as **because** and **so**. They can be clues that help you to know why something happened.

Read the story. Think about what happens and why.

1.
2.
3.

The boys want eggs. **Dad cooks eggs.** **The eggs are ready.**

Read the sentence that tells what happened. Circle the picture that shows why it happened.

What Happened

- The eggs are ready to eat.

Why It Happened

 Tip **When you read, think about how one thing can make another thing happen.**

STRATEGY: Recognizing Cause-and-Effect Relationships

On Your Own — Practicing Comprehension Skills

Read the sentences.
Think about what happens and why.

How Does a Bean Grow?

A bean is a seed you can eat.
You can grow a bean plant.
First, you plant the bean.
Then you water it.
Make sure it gets some light.
Soon you will have a bean plant.
When beans are cooked, you can eat them.

These sentences have two parts.
Read the first part of each sentence.
Then draw a line under the words that
tell what happens next.

1. A bean is a seed, so you can

   <u>plant it.</u>   play catch with it.   yell at it.

2. Because you water the seed,

   a fish grows.   <u>a plant grows.</u>   you grow.

3. When beans are cooked,

   a plant grows.   <u>you can eat them.</u>   throw them away.

Lesson 13

Read the story.
Think about what happens and why.

A Birthday Surprise

Mom and Mina whisper in the kitchen.
Dad is still asleep.
It is his birthday.
Mom and Mina are making a surprise for Dad.
Mina stirs the batter.
Then Mom cooks the pancakes.
When they bring them to Dad,
Mina yells, "Happy Birthday, Dad!"
Dad wakes up with a smile.

These sentences have two parts.
Read the first part of each sentence.
Then draw a line under the words that
tell why something happens.

4. Mom and Mina whisper because

   <u>Dad is asleep.</u>   Dad is working.   Dad is away.

5. They are making a surprise breakfast because it is

   Mom's birthday.   <u>Dad's birthday.</u>   Mina's birthday.

6. Mom will cook the pancakes so

   she can drop them.   Mina can stir them.

   <u>Dad can eat them.</u>

STRATEGY: Recognizing Cause-and-Effect Relationships

Fill in the circle next to the best answer.

7. Why does Dad wake up with a smile?

    ○ He is happy it is raining.

    ● He is happy to have a birthday surprise.

    ○ He does not like pancakes.

Practicing Vocabulary

Draw a line from each clue to the word.

8. get bigger, rise — grow

9. bean, pit — seed

10. hold, carry — bring

11. make, heat — cook

Draw a before and after picture. Write a sentence that tells what happened. Write another sentence that tells why it happened.

Lesson 13

LESSON 14: Real and Make-Believe

Some stories you read are **real**. They could really happen. **Make-believe** stories could **not** really happen. In make-believe stories, animals can talk. People can fly. Anything can happen!

● Only two of these pictures are real. Circle the picture that is not real.

▲ Look at the picture. Then read the questions. Circle the word that answers each question.

● Can raccoons really write letters? Yes (No)
■ Do raccoons really wear clothes? Yes (No)
▲ Is this story real or make-believe? Real (Make-believe)

Tip When you read, think about what could be real and what is make-believe. If something in a story could not really happen, it is make-believe.

STRATEGY: Distinguishing Fantasy from Reality   57

Practicing Comprehension Skills

Read the story. Then read the sentences.
Draw a line under each sentence that is real.
Put an **X** on each sentence that is make-believe.

Jake's Pets

Jake has a dog named Bingo.
He has a kitten named Cleo.
Jake also has a goat named Munch.
Munch likes to eat grass.
Jake likes to eat cookies.
Bingo likes to eat cookies, too!
"Stay away, Bingo," says Jake.
"These cookies are not for you."

1. A ~~dog can read~~.
2. A kitten ~~can use~~ a backpack.
3. <u>A bird can sing.</u>
4. <u>A goat can eat grass.</u>
5. <u>A boy can read a book.</u>
6. A boy can ~~fly like~~ a bird.

Lesson 14

Read the story. Think about what is real and what is make-believe.

Space Race

by Anastasia Suen

Two rockets went into space.
They were racing to a star.
"Can we win?" Dog asked Fox.
"I see the star," Fox told Dog.
"Faster," said Dog. "Here comes Cow!"
Fox and Dog flew over the star.
"We won!" they shouted.

Read each sentence. If it is make-believe, circle the word **Make-believe.** If it is real, circle the word **Real.**

7.	A rocket can go into space.	Make-believe	(Real)
8.	A dog can talk to a fox.	(Make-believe)	Real
9.	A fox and a dog can fly over a star.	(Make-believe)	Real
10.	A star is in space.	Make-believe	(Real)
11.	A cow can fly a rocket.	(Make-believe)	Real
12.	Rockets can go very fast.	Make-believe	(Real)

STRATEGY: Distinguishing Fantasy from Reality

13. Circle the word that tells what kind of story "Space Race" is.

    (Make-believe)   Real

Practicing Vocabulary

Write a word from the box in each sentence.

| star | stay | rockets | kitten |

14. Special pilots fly _____rockets_____ into space.

15. Sam likes to pet his _____kitten_____.

16. At night Jess watches for the first ___star___.

17. When you are sick, you should ___stay___ home.

On another sheet of paper, draw a picture of something that is real and something that is make-believe. Write words to tell about each picture.

Lesson 14

LESSON 15 Using Context Clues

Sometimes when you read, you need to figure out what some words mean.
Look for clues in the pictures.
Other words can also help you.

- Read the first sentence.
  Then circle the word that belongs in the next sentence.

Kelly's smile looks different now.

She lost a _____.

(tooth)   book

What helped you figure out the answer?
If Kelly lost a tooth, her smile would look different.
The words **smile** and **different** are your clues.

Tip When you see a word you do not know, look for clues in the words and pictures.

STRATEGY: Using Context Clues

Practicing Comprehension Skills

Read these sentences.
Write the word that belongs in each sentence.
Use clues to help you.

Animal Teeth

by Wendy Pfeffer

1. Dogs and cats are ___animals___ that have baby teeth.

   | animals |
   | bugs |

2. Animals lose their baby teeth, too. Then they grow bigger teeth just like ___people___ do.

   | chairs |
   | people |

3. Puppies lose their baby teeth when they are about 12 ___weeks___ old.

   | weeks |
   | bags |

4. Then new teeth ___grow___ in.

   | skip |
   | grow |

62 Lesson 15

Read the sentences. Write the word from the box that belongs in each sentence.

What Makes Baby Teeth Fall Out?

by Wendy Pfeffer

bigger   mouth   sets   teeth   room

5. People have two __sets__ of teeth.

6. First, your baby __teeth__ grow in.

7. As you grow, you need __bigger__ teeth.

8. One by one, the baby teeth fall out of your __mouth__.

9. This makes __room__ for the new teeth to grow in.

STRATEGY: Using Context Clues

10. Circle the word that means the same as the underlined word.

It is important to brush your teeth.

(wash)   drink   visit

Practicing Vocabulary

Write the word from the box on the line.

| lose | teeth | mouth | bigger |

11. Nate's __mouth__ is turned up in a big smile.

One of his baby __teeth__ fell out today.

When you __lose__ a tooth, a new tooth will grow in its place. The new tooth that grows in will be __bigger__.

Make a poster on another sheet of paper. Draw a picture that shows how to take care of teeth. Write sentences that tell what to do.

Lesson 15

LESSON 16 Classifying

Some things are alike in some ways. They belong in the same group.

● Look at the pictures.
Circle the two pictures that belong together.

How do the shark and the fish go together? They both swim in water. Does a house swim in water?

▲ Circle the two words that belong together.

(sea)   (water)   land

■ Circle the two sentences that belong together.

Bears live in the forest.
(Many animals live in the sea.)
(You will find all kinds of fish in the sea.)

Tip As you read, think about how things belong together. Then you can put them in a group.

STRATEGY: Classifying   65

On Your Own

Practicing Comprehension Skills

Life at the Pond

Many animals can be found at a pond. Some animals are land animals. Deer, rabbits, and foxes visit the pond for a drink of water.
Other animals are water animals. Fish and turtles swim. Frogs splash.

You read about two groups of animals. One group is Land Animals. The other is Water Animals. Write the name of each animal in the box where it belongs.

| fish | rabbit | frog | deer | fox | turtle |

Land Animals	Water Animals
1. rabbit	4. fish
2. deer	5. frog
3. fox	6. turtle

Lesson 16

Read the story. Look at the picture.

Going to the Seashore

Lisa wanted to swim.
She took a tube.
Ted wanted to play in the sand.
He took a pail.
Mom wanted to sit and read.
She took a book.

At the seashore Lisa found shells.
Ted saw a boat.
Mom fell asleep.

Group some things from Lisa, Ted, and Mom's trip to the seashore.
Write the name of each thing on the line where it belongs.

pail   swim   tube   shells   boat   play

Things to Take	Things to Do	Things to See
1. tube	3. swim	5. shells
2. pail	4. play	6. boat

STRATEGY: Classifying   67

Fill in the circle next to the right answer.

7. What list does Mom's chair belong on?

⬤ **Things to Take**   ◯ **Things to Do**   ◯ **Things to See**

Practicing Vocabulary

Draw a line from the sentence to the word.

8. Water animals live in a _____ .

swim

9. You can swim and fish at the _____ .

found

10. The boy can _____ in deep water.

pond

seashore

11. The girl _____ many shells.

Making the **Reading** *and* **Writing** *Connection*

Use another piece of paper. Draw a picture of some animals that live in the sea.
Write one or two sentences that tell why the animals belong in a group.

68   Lesson 16

LESSON 17: Comparing and Contrasting

Alike means how things are the same.
Different means how things are not the same.

Look at the pictures. Look at the chart.
Think about how the pictures are alike
and different.

	Alike	Different
grows on tree	✔	
color		✔

Sometimes things are alike in one way. They can also be different in another way.

Read these questions. Look at the chart again.
Circle the answer.

● Do apples and pears grow on trees?   (Yes)   No

■ Are apples and pears the same color?   Yes   (No)

Tip When you read, ask yourself if two things are the same or not. Then think about how they are alike and different.

STRATEGY: Comparing and Contrasting   69

Practicing Comprehension Skills

Read the story. How are Sun and Moon alike? How are they different?

Who Is Best?
by Susan L. Roth

Sun and Moon were talking.
"We are both round and live in the sky," said Sun.
"I am hot, and you are cold.
I am big, and you are small. I am best!"
"We both give light," said Moon.
"I help people see at night.
You help people see in the day.
We are both best at what we do."

Write **X** in the boxes to show how Sun and Moon are alike and how they are different.

		Alike	Different
1.	Size		X
2.	Give light	X	
3.	Time when you see them		X
4.	Shape	X	
5.	Live in sky	X	

Lesson 17

Read the story.
Think about how trees and flowers are alike and different.

Trees and Flowers

Trees and flowers are plants.
They grow in the ground.
Trees are big.
Flowers are small.
Trees have green leaves. So do flowers.
Trees have thick bark.
Flowers have thin stems.
Trees and flowers are living things.

Look at the box. Write the words that only tell about trees on the lines under **Trees**. Write the words that only tell about flowers on the lines under **Flowers**. Write the words that tell about trees **and** flowers on the lines under **Both**.

| plant | leaves | big | small | bark | stems |

Trees   **Both**   **Flowers**

6. big   8. plant   10. small

7. bark   9. leaves   11. stems

STRATEGY: Comparing and Contrasting

Decide if the sentence tells only about tree, only about flower, or about both. Circle the answer.

12. It is a living thing. tree flower (both)

Practicing Vocabulary

Write the word from the box that belongs in each group.

talking plants green living

13. flowers, trees, _____plants_____

14. speaking, telling, _____talking_____

15. red, blue, _____green_____

16. being, alive, _____living_____

On another sheet of paper, draw a picture of yourself and a friend.
Write sentences that tell how you are alike and how you are different.

Lesson 17

Author's Purpose

An author is a person who writes a book.
An author has a reason for writing a story.
The author may want to make you laugh.
The author may want to tell you something.

Look at the book.
Draw a circle around the correct answer.

● Who is the author of this book?

(Fred Green)
Fred Baseball
Fred Games

■ What do you think this book is about?

food   (games)   animals

▲ Why do you think the author wrote this book?

to be funny   to sell games   (to tell about games)

Tip Read the name of the story or book. Look at the pictures. Then think about why the author wrote the book.

STRATEGY: Recognizing Author's Purpose   73

Practicing Comprehension Skills

Read the sentences.
Think about why the author wrote "Hang Time."

Hang Time

by Kelly Brice

To play Hang Time, you need a ball.
Start counting when you toss it in the air.
Stop counting when you catch it.
Remember the number.
Let a friend toss the ball in the air.
See whose ball stays up the longest.

Draw a line under the answer.

1. Why did the author write Hang Time?

    to tell about clocks   to tell about Hang Time

    to make people sing songs

2. Why did the author write the words, "Remember the number"?

    to help you dance   to teach you numbers

    so you will know whose ball was up the longest

3. Which book tells you about Hang Time?

    Animal Stories   Ball Games   Dogs and Cats

74 Lesson 18

Read this story.
Think about why the author wrote it.

The Great Catch

"Toss the ball to Pete!" Max called out.
"He'll drop it!" Kim said. "He always drops it!"
Pete felt bad. He wanted to be a good player.
He didn't want to let his team down.
Kim tossed the ball to Pete.
Pete watched the ball sail in the air.
He held up his glove. The ball fell in.
Pete waved the ball in the air and smiled.

Fill in the circle next to the answer.

4. Why does the author write that the ball fell into Pete's glove?

    ○ so we know that Pete dropped the ball

    ○ so we know the ball fell on the ground

    ● so we know the ball landed in Pete's glove

5. Why does the author write that Pete smiled?

    ○ so we know that Kim is mad

    ● so we know that Pete is happy

    ○ so we know that Max is sad

STRATEGY: Recognizing Author's Purpose

Draw a line under the best answer.

6. Why do you think the author wrote "The Great Catch"?

   To make you cry.

   To make you smile.

   To tell you who to play with.

Practicing Vocabulary

Draw a line from the word to the group where it belongs.

stop	**7.** think about again, recall
remember	**8.** fall, let go
sail	**9.** halt, quit
drop	**10.** move, fly

Making the Reading and Writing Connection

Use another sheet of paper. Draw a picture of a game you like to play. Write some sentences that tell how to play the game.

Lesson 19 Plot

Every story has a **plot**.
The plot is what happens in the story.
A plot has a beginning, a middle, and an end.

These pictures tell a story.

Beginning   Middle   End

Fill in the circle next to the correct answer.

● **What happened at the beginning?**

  ○ They went to the store.   ● They went on a picnic.

■ **What happened in the middle?**

  ● It began to rain.   ○ It began to snow.

▲ **What happened at the end?**

  ○ They went outside.   ● They ate in the car.

Tip — When you read a story, try to figure out what happened at the beginning, middle, and end. Then you will know the plot.

STRATEGY: Literary Elements: Plot   77

Practicing Comprehension Skills

Read the story. Think about what happens in the beginning, middle, and end.

Going to a Pet Show

Rex is getting a bath.
"We're going to the pet show," Jack said.
"Rex will win the cleanest dog prize!"
said Dan.
Then Rex ran in the mud.
Jack and Dan took him to the pet show anyway.
Later Dan said, "I knew Rex would win a prize."
"Rex won the Dirty Dog prize!" Jack said.
The boys laughed. Rex barked.

1. Write 1, 2, or 3 next to each picture to show what happened at the beginning, middle, and end of the story.

_1_   _3_   _2_

2. What prize does Rex win?
   Fill in the circle next to the answer.

   ○ Clean Dog   ○ Fast Dog   ● Dirty Dog

Lesson 19

Read the story. Think about what happens at the beginning, middle, and end.

Space Dog

Boots was hungry.
He looked for food everywhere.
He even looked on a spaceship!
When Mom saw Boots, she smiled.
Then she gave Boots a big bone.
"You're going to be the first dog on the moon!" she said.

Fill in the circle next to the correct answer.

3. What happens at the beginning?

4. What happens in the middle?

STRATEGY: Literary Elements: Plot

5. What happens at the end of the story?
   Fill in the circle next to the picture.

Practicing Vocabulary

Write a word from the box on each line.

6. I think _____you're_____ nice.

7. The _____hungry_____ dog ate a bone.

8. _____We're_____ going away today.

9. The dog won a _____prize_____.

| hungry |
| we're |
| prize |
| you're |

On another sheet of paper, draw three pictures. Show the beginning, the middle, and the end of a trip you want to go on. Write a sentence to tell about each picture.

80 Lesson 19

LESSON 20 Character

Characters are the people authors write about in stories.
Authors tell what the characters do.
Authors tell how the characters feel, too.

Read the story. Think about the characters.

Megan likes to play with her toys.
She pretends they are her friends.
"Isn't this fun?" she asks them.
Then she laughs.

Fill in the circle next to the correct answer.

● Who is the character in this story?

　● a girl　　○ a boy　　○ a butterfly

■ What does the character like to do?

　○ go to sleep　　● play with her toys　　○ read maps

▲ How does the character feel?

　○ sad　　○ tired　　● happy

Tip When you read, think about who the characters are. Think about what the characters do and how they feel.

STRATEGY: Literary Elements: Character　　81

On Your Own

Practicing Comprehension Skills

Read the poem. Think about who the main character is.

Pete the Knight

by J. Patrick Lewis

"I want to be a knight," said Pete.
"I'll go to ask the King.
I want to be a knight because
I can do anything.
I ride a horse. I read big books.
I go to school. I sing!"

Fill in the circle next to the correct answer.

1. Who is the main character?

    ○ Megan   ● Pete   ○ Jake

2. What does the character want to be?

    ○ a cowboy   ○ a teacher   ● a knight

3. What will the character do to become a knight?

    ● Ask the King.   ○ Run a race.   ○ Play a game.

Lesson 20

Read the poem. Think about who the main character is.

Pete Meets the King

by J. Patrick Lewis

The King was brave. The King was kind.
He walked along the street.
"Good day. How do you do?"
he'd say to people he would meet.
He knew today he'd meet a knight.
The knight he met was Pete!

Draw a line under the correct answer.

4. Who is the most important character?

   Pete   a horse   <u>the King</u>

5. What does the King do that shows he likes people?

   The King asks people to visit his castle.

   The King shows people his horse.

   <u>The King says, "Good day" to people.</u>

6. How do you think the King feels as he walks down the street?

   sleepy   silly   <u>happy</u>

STRATEGY: Literary Elements: Character

7. Which words tell about the King?
Write the words on the line.

tired and hungry	brave and kind	loud and wild

The king is _____ brave and kind _____.

Practicing Vocabulary

Draw a line from the sentence to the word.

8. The ____ rode on his horse. — **anything**

9. He would do ____ the king asked. — **knight**

10. He was very ____. — **brave**

11. He ____ the king was his friend. — **knew**

On another sheet of paper, draw a picture of a story character you like. Then write two or three sentences about the character.

Lesson 20

Setting

The **setting** is when and where a story happens. Pictures can help you tell where a story happens. So can words.

Look at the pictures. Draw a line under the words that tell you where or when the story happens.

● at the zoo

   at the beach

■ at night

   in the daytime

▲ Draw a circle around the picture that shows something that happened a long time ago.

Tip When you read, think about when and where a story happens.

STRATEGY: Literary Elements: Setting   85

Practicing Comprehension Skills

Read the story. Think about where and when the story happens.

A Fish Story

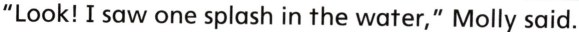

Molly and her dad went fishing.
"This river is full of fish," Dad said.
"Look! I saw one splash in the water," Molly said.
"We'll catch our dinner," Dad told her.
Molly and her dad fished all day.
That night they ate fish for dinner.

Fill in the circle next to the answer.

1. Where does this story happen?

   ○ in school   ● on a river   ○ in a city

2. When does this story happen?

   ○ in the winter   ○ a long time ago   ● in the summer

3. What clue helped you tell when the story happens? Underline the answer.

   <u>Molly and Dad are wearing bathing suits.</u>

   Molly and Dad are wearing coats.

   Molly and Dad are very cold.

Lesson 21

Read the story. Think about when and where the story happens.

A Trip to the Zoo

It was windy outside.
"I'll wear my jacket," Lily said.
Lily and her mom rode on a bus.
They saw seals.
They saw big cats, too.
A cloud covered the sun.
Lily was glad she had her jacket.

Draw a circle around the correct answer.

4. Where does this story happen?

   at home   (at the zoo)   at school

5. When does this story happen?

   in the rain   on a hot day   (on a chilly day)

Fill in the circle next to the correct answer.

6. How can you tell where the story happens?

   ○ A cloud covered the sun.

   ● Lily and her mom see different animals.

   ○ It is windy outside.

STRATEGY: Literary Elements: Setting   87

7. What in the story helps you tell when the story happens? Fill in the circle.

○ Lily and her mom ride a bus.

○ Lily and her mom go to the zoo.

● Lily is glad she wore her jacket.

Practicing Vocabulary

Find a word in the box that matches each clue. Write it on the line.

| I'll | windy | we'll | dinner |

___we'll___ **8.** we will

___I'll___ **9.** I will

___windy___ **10.** breezy

___dinner___ **11.** meal

Use another sheet of paper. Write a story about something two friends do together. Be sure to tell when your story happens. Tell where it happens, too.

88 Lesson 21

Alphabetizing

The letters in the alphabet are in ABC order. ABC order can make things easy to find.

Point to each letter. Say its name.
Think about the order of the letters.

a b c d e f g   h i j k l m n o p   q r s t u v   w x y z

Write the missing letters on the lines.

● e __*f*__ g   j __*k*__ l   p __*q*__ r

■ c __*d*__ e __*f*__   r __*s*__ t __*u*__ v

▲ u __*v*__ w   x __*y*__

Tip Say the abc's to yourself. Think about the order of the letters. Then you will know how to put things in ABC order.

STRATEGY: Alphabetizing   89

Practicing Comprehension Skills

Read the story. Think about how the children will use ABC order.

A Color March

Meg put on a green hat.
"This is my size!" she said.
Alex put on an orange coat.
Holly put on a yellow dress.
"Now we can march," said Holly.
"We'll march with colors in ABC order!"

How will the children use ABC order?
They will put the color words in ABC order.

Circle the words that are in ABC order.

1. yellow   green   orange

    green   yellow   orange

    (green   orange   yellow)

2. (Alex   Holly   Meg)

    Holly   Alex   Meg

    Meg   Holly   Alex

90 Lesson 22

Read the story. Find out how these children use ABC order.

An ABC Rainbow

We paint with our favorite colors.
Ann paints with red.
Mike paints with blue.
Jim paints with yellow.
We put the pictures in a line.
Look at our ABC rainbow!

Draw a line under the first letter of each color name. Then write 1, 2, and 3 to put each group of color words in ABC order.

3.

__3__ yellow   __1__ blue   __2__ red

4.

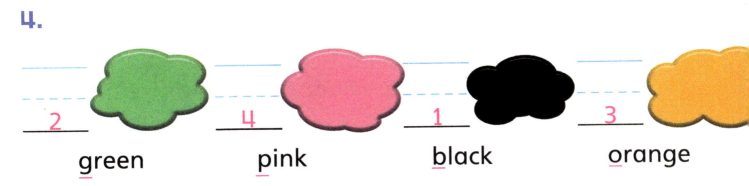

__2__   __4__   __1__   __3__
green   pink   black   orange

STRATEGY: Alphabetizing   91

Put the words in ABC order to write a sentence.

painting   love   rainbows   children   All

5. All children love painting rainbows.

Practicing Vocabulary

Draw a line from the word to the clue it matches.

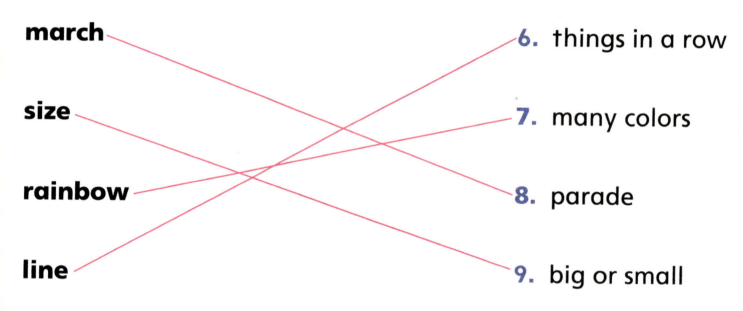

march

size

rainbow

line

6. things in a row

7. many colors

8. parade

9. big or small

Get four sheets of paper. Use a different color to draw a picture on each sheet. Write the color name. Then put the colors in ABC order.

92   Lesson 22

LESSON 23 Picture Maps

A **picture map** shows you what a place looks like. It can also show you how to go from place to place.

This picture map shows a park.

● Circle what is at the front of the park.

■ Circle where you can feed the ducks.

 Tip Each picture on a picture map shows a place. Read a picture map by looking at each picture. Labels on the map may also help you.

STRATEGY: Reading a Picture Map   93

Practicing Study Skills

Read the story.
Look at the picture map.

A Place to Play

This is where I like to play.
I climb up and up. Then I slide down.
I build a sand castle.
I swing so high I can touch the sky.
Mom waves from the bench.

Draw a line under the correct answer.

1. What does the picture map show?

   farm   <u>playground</u>   town

Read each sentence.
Then show the place on the map.

2. Draw a ◯ circle around where you can swing.

3. Draw a △ triangle around where you can slide.

4. Draw a ☐ box around where you can play in the sand.

Read the poem. Look at the picture map.

Camp Fun

The Green family goes to Camp Fun.
At Camp Fun they ride, fish, and run.
First they work. Then they play.
They put up their tent in one day!
Soon they are tired. They want to eat.
Can you guess where they will meet?

Draw a circle around the correct answer.

5. Where will the Green family sleep?

　　(tent)　　boat　　tree

6. Where will the Greens fish?

　　tree　　table　　(lake)

7. Where will the Green family meet to eat?

　　boat　　(table)　　tent

8. Fill in the circle next to the things you can do at Camp Fun.

　　● eat　　● fish　　○ shop

STRATEGY: Reading a Picture Map   95

Write your answer on the line.

9. What would you like to do at Camp Fun?

_____

Answers will vary.
_____

Practicing Vocabulary

Draw a line from the word to the group where it belongs.

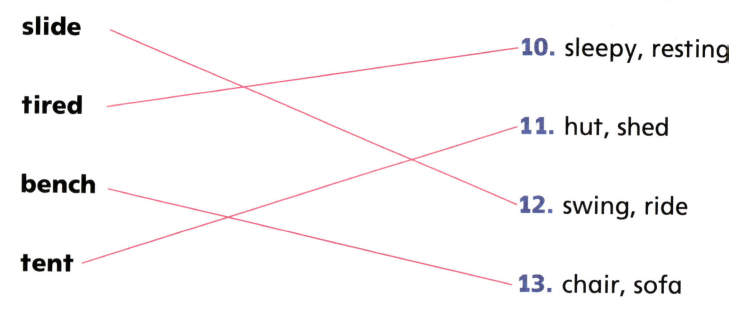

slide

tired

bench

tent

10. sleepy, resting

11. hut, shed

12. swing, ride

13. chair, sofa

Use another piece of paper. Draw a picture map of a place where you have fun. First, draw pictures on your map. Then write a word that tells about each picture.

96 Lesson 23

LESSON 24 Picture and Bar Graphs

A **picture graph** or **bar graph** is a picture that tells a number story. Picture or bar graphs make it easy to count and compare things.

Mr. Lopez ordered four trumpets, two tubas, and three trombones for the school band.

This bar graph shows what Mr. Lopez ordered.

Horns for the Band

Trumpets						
Tubas						
Trombones						
	1	2	3	4	5	6

Use the bar graph to answer each question. Circle the correct answer.

● How many trumpets were ordered? 1 2 3 (4)

■ How many tubas? 1 (2) 3 4

▲ How many trombones? 1 2 (3) 4

Tip Read the words and numbers on the bar graph. Find what you want to count. Then tell how many.

STRATEGY: Using Bar Graphs 97

Practicing Study Skills

Read the poem. Then look at the bar graph.

Flags in the Parade

The parade goes down the street.
Green and blue flags fly.
The flags go up.
The flags go down.
The marching feet go by.
Yellow flags and red flags, too.
I can see them. So can you!

Read each sentence.
Circle **Yes** or **No**.

1. The parade has six red flags.

   (Yes)   No

2. The parade has three blue flags.

   Yes   (No)

3. There are more red flags than green flags.

   (Yes)   No

4. There are more yellow flags than green flags.

   Yes   (No)

98   Lesson 24

Read the story. Look at the bar graph.

How Many Songs?

My class has a spring show.
We sing songs for our families.
The girls sing two songs.
The boys sing three songs.
Brad sings two songs by himself.
We sing some songs together.

How Many Songs?

	1	2	3	4	5	6
the girls	▓	▓				
the boys	▓	▓	▓			
Brad	▓	▓				
together	▓	▓	▓			

Write the number on the line.

5. Everyone sings ___3___ songs together.

6. Brad sings ___2___ songs by himself.

STRATEGY: Using Bar Graphs   99

Look at the bar graph again.
Write the number on the line.

7. At the spring show, the children sing ___10___ songs.

Practicing Vocabulary

Write the word from the box that matches each clue.

___show___ **8.** singing and dancing on stage

___families___ **9.** moms, dads, sisters, brothers

___go___ **10.** move

___parade___ **11.** people marching down the street

> go
> parade
> show
> families

On another piece of paper, make a bar graph. Show what you and your friends might play in a band.

Lesson 24

Level A Glossary

A   **again** (ə gen´) once more; a second time

another (ə nuth´ər) one more

anything (en´ē thiŋ) any thing; something, no matter what

B   **balloon** (bə loon´) a brightly colored rubber bag that is blown up with air

bears (berz) large animals with shaggy fur and short tails

bench (bench) a long, hard seat for a few people

bigger (big´ər) of greater size; larger

bird (bᴜrd) an animal that is covered with feathers and has two feet and two wings

blimp (blimp) an airship shaped somewhat like an egg

brave (brāv) not afraid of facing danger, pain, or trouble

bring (briŋ) to carry somewhere

C   **cake** (kāk) a baked food that is made from a sweet batter

captain (kap´tən) the person in charge of a ship

catch (kach) to get by a hook, trap, or other tool

cook (kᴏͻk) to prepare food for eating by using heat

cubs (kubz) baby lions, bears, whales, or other animals

D   **different** (dif´ər ənt or dif´rənt) not the same

dinner (din´ər) the main meal of the day

dream (drēm) thoughts, pictures, or feelings that you have while you sleep

drop (dräp) to fall or let fall

F   **families** (fam´ə lēz) groups made up of one or two parents and all their children

first (fᴜrst) before anyone or anything else

fish (fish) animals with fins and gills that live in water

flies (flɪz) moves through the air by using wings

flowers (flou´ərz) the parts of a plant that have colored petals

fly (flɪ) to move through the air by using wings

found (found) discovered

G   **go** (gō) to move along or pass from one place to another

green (grēn) having the color of growing grass

grow (grō) to make something get bigger

H   **help** (help) to do something that is needed; to make things easier for someone

hive (hɪv) a box where bees live

101

huge (hyŏŏj) very large

hungry (huŋ´grē) wanting or needing food

I'll (īl) I will

kitchen (kich´ən) a room for cooking food

kitten (kit´n) a young cat

knew (nŏŏ or nyŏŏ) was sure

knight (nīt) a man in the Middle Ages who was honored by the king

letters (let´ərz) written messages, usually sent by mail

line (līn) a row of persons or things

living (liv´iŋ) having life; alive; not dead

lose (lŏŏz) to not have something anymore

made (mād) created or put together

march (märch) to walk with regular, steady steps as soldiers do

mouth (mouth) the opening in someone's head through which food is taken in and sounds are made

nuts (nuts) dry fruits with hard shells

parade (pə rād´) people marching in a group

pick (pik) to choose or select

pilot (pī´lət) a person who flies an airplane

plane (plān) an aircraft that is kept up by the air on its wings

plants (plants) living things that cannot move around by themselves

plates (plāts) dishes used for food

pond (pänd) a small lake

prize (prīz) something that is given to the winner of a contest or game

quit (kwit) to stop doing something

rainbow (rān´bō) a curved band of many colors across the sky

raincoats (rān´kōts) coats that protect people from the rain

reads (rēdz) understands the meaning of something written

remember (rē mem´bər) to be careful not to forget; to think of again

ring (riŋ) a thin band worn on the finger

rockets (räk´əts) long, narrow machines that fly or help things fly

sail (sāl) to move in a smooth and easy way

sand (sand) the tiny grains that make up the ground of a beach or a desert

school (skŏŏl) a place for teaching and learning

seashore (sē´shôr) land by the sea

seed (sēd) the part of a plant that can grow into a new plant

shade (shād) to protect from light and heat

shoes (sho͞oz) coverings for the feet

show (shō) a performance of a play or music

size (sīz) how large or small a thing is

sky (skī) the upper part of the air around Earth

sled (sled) a low platform on runners that is used for riding over snow

sleep (slēp) to be at rest with the eyes closed

slide (slīd) to slip

smell (smel) to notice an odor through the nose; an odor that is noticed by the nose

snow (snō) soft, white flakes that form from tiny drops of water that freeze in the upper air and fall to earth

spider (spī´dər) a small animal with eight legs and a body made up of two parts

star (stär) an object in space that shines by its own light and is seen as a point of light in the night sky

stay (stā) to keep on being in the same place

stop (stäp) to keep from going on

swim (swim) to move through the water by moving the arms and legs

T **talking** (tôk´iŋ) saying words; speaking

teeth (tēth) white, bony parts that grow in the mouth and are used to bite and chew

tent (tent) a shelter made of material that is stretched over poles and attached to the ground

tired (tīrd) needing sleep or rest

U **use** (yo͞oz) to put into action

W **warm** (wôrm) keeping the body heat in

water (wôt´ər) a liquid that has no color and falls as rain to fill the oceans, rivers, and lakes

we'll (wēl) we will

we're (wir) we are

whale (hwāl or wāl) a very large animal that lives in the sea and looks something like a fish

why (hwī or wī) for what reason?

windy (win´dē) with a lot of wind

worm (wɜrm) a small, creeping animal that has a soft, slender body and no legs

Y **you're** (yo͝or or yo͞or) you are